VOLUME II

Beyond The Veil

VOLUME II

Beyond The Veil

Lee Nelson

6 7 8 9 10

ISBN: 1-55517-172-8

Printed and distributed in the United States by:

Table of Contents

Publisher's Foreword

In the Publisher's Foreword of *Beyond the Veil, Volume One,* we mentioned we had two fears that seem to override all others when a project of this nature is attempted; first, the fear of not being believed; and second, the fear that others will esteem the project as simply commercial. These projects have been so fulfilling spiritually, we hope all of you get a sense, by reading these experiences, of what we have been through.

Like the accounts in *Volume One,* these stories in *Volume II* are also extremely personal and private. We have encountered much less reticence from people on this volume, however, than we did with *Volume One.* We regard this as extremely positive. These narratives are so sweet, uplifting, comforting, and motivating it would be a shame to not have them available. We feel that these people who have taken the risk of sharing their experiences will sometime reap great satisfaction. They have told the truth and without fear.

As we mentioned before, these narratives are not meant to be read and discussed from a doctrinal point of view. Such an attempt would probably be futile. Please read them simply for whatever benefit may be individually appropriate. We ask again, specifically, that these stories not be passed on orally from friend to friend but only read and pondered in private.

If, after reading these stories, you are aware of a similar account, experienced by you or a loved one, that would be an appropriate addition to the growing body of evidence that the human soul lives beyond the grave, we invite you to tell us about the account on cassette tape and send it to us for possible publication in a future volume of *Beyond the Veil*. Please include appropriate addresses and phone numbers in case we wish to obtain permission to publish the story.

Send to:

Beyond the Veil
Cedar Fort Incorporated
1182 N. Industrial Park Dr.
Orem, Utah 84057

INTRODUCTION

Since I started work on this *Volume II Beyond the Veil,* I have been amazed at the wide acceptance of these kinds of experiences. In a society laced with atheism and unquestionable materialism, at a time when interest in religion in general seems at best luke warm it might seem strange that many of the best-selling books deal with so-called spiritual after life experiences. Of course, I'm referring to society as a whole.

I think one of the reasons for the keen interest in after life experiences is the undeniable strength of some of the stories or incidents—like the Swiss architect whose serious car accident was reported in a recent issue of a nursing journal. The accident occurred on a narrow mountain road the day of a national soccer championship.

After the paramedics declared the man dead, they covered him with a blanket and left him on a stretcher. Meanwhile the emergency crew began clearing away the wreckage of his car, which was blocking the road and tying up traffic for miles.

The architect said that as he rose in the air above his body, he could somehow hear the complaining and swearing of the fans who were missing the opening of the soccer match because of the traffic delay. Nobody seemed to care that a man had just died.

Then he became aware of a lone female voice praying for the accident victim. Not sure if the victim shared her faith in Christ, she prayed that whoever his god was, that God would help him.

Touched by her concern, the architect vowed that her prayers would be answered. He decided to return to his body, was able to do it, and somehow made himself known to the paramedics.

Nine hard months of recovery later he begged his doctor to help him find the woman who had prayed for him. He didn't know the woman's name, and since there had been hundreds of cars in the traffic jam at the time of the accident, the doctor said finding the woman would be impossible—until the patient told the doctor he had seen and remembered the woman's license plate number.

In the introduction to Volume I of *Beyond the Veil,* I mentioned I was praying for my own beyond the veil experience. I suppose after interviewing all those people and helping write their stories, I got the feeling that I would like to step beyond the veil myself, even if for only a brief moment. Of course there's always the worry that if you managed to get there, they might not allow you to come back.

When my publisher read the part in the introduction to Volume I about my desire to have my own experience he said he was going to delete it.

"Why?" I asked.

"Readers who don't know you won't understand your sense of humor, that you are only joking," he explained.

"I wasn't joking," I said, explaining that I made the comment in all seriousness. He left it in, and I did get at least one letter from a concerned reader who chastised me for having such a wish.

Right after the book came off the press last year I thought for a brief moment my wish for a beyond the veil experience would be realized. I was on a wind-swept plateau in central Nevada where my friend Jeff Wolf and I were engaged in a so-called research project for my next *Storm Testament*-series book about Walkara, the Ute Indian from Spanish Fork Canyon who became the greatest horse thief in the history of the American West.

Jeff and I were camped off one edge of the plateau. Every morning at first light, and in the evening too, we would venture onto the tree-less table to look for deer. Our object was to kill a big buck from horseback with bows and arrows, the way some Indians used to do it.

The plateau was about three miles across, at an elevation of about 11,000 feet. The ground was covered with short grass and some brush. While there were no trees, there were some rocky places and steep hills and ledges which made chasing difficult, or at least challenging—and the wary deer seemed to lead us into those difficult places whenever a chase was on. I was riding Dan, my speedy quarter horse, and Jeff was mounted on Tom, a tall, black thoroughbred that had been raced on the track as a two-year-old.

Typically, we would ride the horses to a more or less secluded meadow near a high outcropping of rock from which we could see a large portion of the plateau. After hobbling the horses in the meadow, we would crawl cautiously to the most advantageous location in the rocks, set up our spotting scope, take out our binoculars, and begin looking for bucks, being very slow and cautious with our movements so as not to attract the attention of the deer.

On the particular evening in question, we had just crawled to our favorite vantage point when we saw 20 deer, the most we had ever seen from there before—and all but one were bucks. The deer were grazing along the edge of the plateau, a cliff about 400 yards away. They were moving slowly westward towards our favorite chasing location.

We watched them for an hour or so, focusing most of our attention on the biggest of the bucks—and there were several in the trophy category with antlers high and wide.

Our plan was simple. As soon as the browsing deer reached the desired spot, one of us would circle around to the far side, then from opposite directions we would close in on the deer, Jeff from the east, me from the west, both riding along the edge of the cliff which blocked a northward exit by the deer. With Jeff and I essentially blocking off the east and west exits, the deer theoretically would be forced to run southward up a gentle valley where it would be ideal to chase them. Once headed up the valley, it was over a mile before the deer could reach any effective cover—ledges, thick brush, pine forests, etc.

Ten minutes later as I began closing in from the west along the edge of the cliff, four bucks we hadn't seen from our earlier lookout point jumped up and charged towards the deer we had been watching. Not wanting them to be too far in front of me when they started the others stampeding, I eased my horse into a fast trot.

Reaching the top of a small hill I could see all 25 deer milling in a circle near the edge of the cliff. They had already seen Jeff closing in from the east, and knew I was coming from the west. They seemed reluctant to head up the little valley where it would be over a mile before any effective cover could be reached. I eased my horse into a gallop. My bow was in my left hand, an arrow already notched on the string.

Suddenly, two or three deer streaked south into the open valley. The rest followed. My horse didn't need any coaxing to stretch out into a full gallop. When he saw the deer, he began snorting like an excited stud horse.

The chase was on. There was no stopping now. The adrenalin was flowing freely in the deer, the horses, and the men.

Closing on the deer at an angle, I soon found myself in the middle of them. Like sheep, they seemed determined to stay together, even with a man on horseback running with them. I resisted several easy shots at nice deer, my eye on the biggest buck on the far side.

With racing deer in front and behind, I moved through them until I was about 15 yards from the biggest buck and closing quickly. I dropped the reins and began to pull back the bow string.

Suddenly, the big buck began to turn left into a field of rocks. Not wanting him to separate himself from the herd I reined my horse in a little, allowing the deer the hope that if he straightened out, he would be able to pull ahead of me and regain the company of his friends. He did just that.

I was closing the gap again, about 30 yards behind the desired target, when the herd of deer suddenly reached the crest of a hill and began a gentle downward run. They now had a small advantage on me because I was still running uphill. My horse was rapidly tiring, and so were the deer. The hind legs of the big buck were flipping out to the left side with each lunge.

Once I reached the top of the hill, I began closing the gap again, touching my horse with the spurs to give him a little extra encouragement. Slowly, we began gaining again on the tiring deer.

I was almost close enough to begin shooting when the big buck suddenly dropped out of sight. I hadn't seen the approaching drop-off, something like that steep downhill in the *Snowy River* movies. The buck had gone over the edge, and my horse was determined to follow. There wasn't time to stop, and if I tried I might distract him from concentrating where he was placing his feet, so over we went, just as Jeff and his horse caught us. All of us went over together. There was too much brush and too many rocks, and the downward angle was too steep.

I remember for a brief moment regretting that I had prayed for my own beyond the veil experience. When it came right down to it, I really didn't want to give up this earthly existence, even for a few moments. I don't think I was any more afraid of death than I had been earlier. I just didn't want my horse to go down.

My horse stumbled, and I thought, "This is it! My friends on the other side, here I come!"

But I didn't. Somehow, the horse was able to regain his footing without going down. We veered to one side, and gradually came to a stop as the buck clattered across a bed of rocks and over a ledge, Jeff and the tall black still in close pursuit.

Now I began to worry about Jeff and what I would tell his wife if I had to bring him home prone over the back of a horse. But a little while later Jeff came riding up out of the ledges. The buck had safely escaped. We laughed about the great stories he would have to tell his posterity about the time he outran and outsmarted the two mounted archers.

After thinking about it, I concluded the Lord probably didn't want me to have my own out-of-body experience, at least not at that time. Possibly I didn't need such an experience, at least not yet. And I have to admit, that after that wild ride across a wind-swept mountain top, I no longer yearn for an experience to plunge me beyond the veil, even if for only a brief moment or two, though I am convinced we all go there at the moment of death, and that we need not be afraid.

At the end of the first volume, we invited readers to submit narrations of personal beyond the veil experiences for consideration in future volumes. Immediately following publication of the first volume the stories began pouring in, from all over—some written up, some on cassette tape.

As I began reading and listening to the stories, I was amazed at the variety of content and experience. The subject was not getting old, or boring. Not in the least.

A lady from California gave the book to her husband for his birthday. She described how he had stayed up much of the night reading—and how overwhelmed he had been by the stories. While reading the book he had started crying, believing his own life would be threatened in the near future. The next morning he told his wife he was going to buy a second life insurance policy, which he did. Three weeks later he was shot 12 times by an armed assailant. (See the Jill Heasley story in this volume.)

In the story of Ella Jensen's near-death experience she describes going beyond the veil and meeting her Uncle Hance who had disappeared years earlier while fishing on the Snake River in Idaho. While the other angelic personages she saw were wearing white, Uncle Hance was wearing a jumper with overalls and gum boots, the same clothing he was wearing at the time of his disappearance, adding support to the belief that the dead often appear to the living in the same clothing they were wearing at the time of death to make it easier for the living to recognize them.

I related this incident to Barbara Jensen, a neighbor who recalled a similar happening in her family after the death of her father of a heart attack at age 62. Barbara had been present soon after the heart attack began and had tried desperately to help her father resume breathing until medical help arrived. By the time her father was on life support systems at the hospital with his heartbeat resumed, there was no sign of any brain waves. The life support systems were turned off and he was allowed to die.

Barbara and the rest of the family were naturally distraught over the death. He was too young to die, they thought, and they wondered if there had been something more they could have done to help prevent the death.

The distress and unrest continued for several weeks until one day Barbara's sister-in-law Pat Hall called to tell Barbara about a dream she had had, a very realistic dream. She was behind the house painting when Barbara's father casually walked around the corner of the house to tell her that everything was all right with him.

"Tell them I had to go," he said. "Everything is fine."

Pat went on to say how vivid and clear the dream had been, like it was more than just a dream.

"What was he wearing?" Barbara asked.

"Khaki work pants and that blue Hawaiian shirt," Pat explained, referring to a shirt Barbara's sister, Linda, had made for her father on his birthday. Everyone, except the father, thought the shirt was ugly.

Barbara was taken back by Pat's description of what her father was wearing—the same clothing he had been wearing at the time of his death, yet Pat didn't know that. When asked about it, Pat said she didn't know what he had been wearing the day he died, only what he had been wearing in the dream.

The fact that the father was wearing the same clothes in the dream that he had been wearing at the time of his death—something Pat was not aware of—convinced Barbara that the dream was more than just a dream, that her father really was doing well, that it had been time for him to go.

Another theme that recurs in several of the new stories, is the yardsticks for judgment that some subjects experience when they pass beyond the veil.

Wealth, power, position in the church, even attendance at church meetings didn't seem to matter—only what one did to improve conditions and lighten the burdens of others. Christian service and charity were far ahead of anything else in winning approval and peace for those entering the world of spirits.

As I began work on this volume, I was amazed at the vast abundance of spiritual experiences people were having, many having something to do with that thin veil separating us from our spirit brothers and sisters. It is refreshing to know that miracles are happening every day—answered prayers, spiritual manifestations, visions, healings through the laying on of hands, even the dead being raised. Everywhere, it seems, I see more and more people making important decisions based on how they feel after earnest prayer.

I hope this book, in its own small way, can add a little strength or momentum to the groundswell of what could be called a spiritual awakening. Take a look around. It's happening.

Lee Nelson

Chapter One

Sidelined

by Kent Johnson

My first wife, Carol, always said logging was a good way to get killed. But when I was out of work the summer of 1987, it seemed like the best way to provide for my family.

Years earlier I was in the army. I had been commissioned as a chaplain and was stationed at Fort Sill, Oklahoma, with Carol and our four children. When the mother of Carol's friend died from breast cancer, Carol became concerned about some soreness she had been experiencing. She had it checked. They found a malignant tumor so large the doctors gave us little hope. Carol went through the mastectomy, the chemo-therapy and the radiation treatments, but died in December of 1984.

I've always felt that Carol was somehow instrumental in my meeting and marrying Crystal. Crystal moved into our old Orem, Utah, ward with her four girls after Carol and I left for Fort Sill. Following Carol's death, the bishop introduced Crystal and I and even double dated with us. We were married a short time later.

My older brother, Mike, had done more logging than I and helped purchase a nice stand of trees in the Payette National Forest. The trees averaged six thousand pounds, were sixty to seventy feet tall and eighteen to twenty-four inches in diameter.

Mike and I and a friend, Art Troutner, were logging the sale on May 22, 1987. About 11:30 a.m., Art came over to where I was and asked for help on a tree. He had wedged it on the back cut trying to get it to fall uphill, but it had bound up his saw.

When I examined the tree a little more closely, I found a pitch seam on the uphill side. That usually indicated the tree was unsound and could split, creating what we called a "barber chair". If the tree splits as it falls, it will sometimes kick the base of the tree out from the stump leaving a slab on the stump resembling a high back barber chair. It is a very dangerous situation.

I told Art to start cutting with my saw. When the tree started falling, he was to run along the slope of the hill perpendicular to the fall of the tree. I would pull his saw out as soon as it became loose and run the other way.

The tree split as I suspected. Art ran, I got the chain saw out, dropped it and ran in the opposite direction. The tree, however, did not fall exactly as we had expected. As we measured later, I was twenty-eight feet from the stump when the tree split and barber-chaired. The base of the tree trunk, sharpened by the chainsaw cuts, leaped from the stump in my direction spearing me in the back at shoulder height. I felt my back snap as I was driven into the ground face-first, filling my mouth and eyes full of dirt. The tree trunk then slammed down on top of me.

As the weight of the tree crushed down on me, I felt my spirit leave my body. I knew immediately I was dead. There was no question. It was all over.

The first emotion I felt was terror. I did not want it to be over. I wanted to be with my wife and kids. I had things to do, things to accomplish. The terror was soon replaced by disappointment.

When I was in high school I was starting lineman on our undefeated football team. I've thought the disappointment I felt at the accident was probably like being pulled out of a championship football game, put on the sidelines and told you were through playing. For the rest of the game you had to watch. I did not want to watch, I wanted to play. I wanted to be in the action.

Following the accident I felt a great acceleration of speed like I was traveling very fast through the darkness that had now closed in around me. I also noticed that my mind was very alert and crystal clear. I could comprehend anything. I was not constrained by my body. I noticed that the pain was completely gone and I had no discomfort at all.

The earlier fear and disappointment were replaced by peace and a definite feeling of well-being. Everything was okay. Everything was just as it should be. As this feeling came, I emerged out of the darkness and became aware that I was not alone. I felt the presence of people before I actually saw anyone.

As I looked, I saw my first wife, Carol, my mother who had died in 1977 from a stroke, and my Grandfather who had died in 1974. He had been in his late eighties or early nineties when he died.

It seemed very natural that Granddad should be there. He was always our family patriarch. He was always very firm and stalwart in his testimony of the gospel. When he was younger he had been friends with President David O. McKay. My mother suffered from illnesses when she was young, and Granddad had once asked President McKay to administer to her. In his blessing he told Mother that she would live to raise her children. My youngest sister was in college the year she died.

Being reunited with my loved ones, especially my first wife filled me with the greatest feelings of love, acceptance and overwhelming sweetness. I was reminded of Lehi's dream and his description of the love of God.

He described it as *fruit ...desirable to make one happy* and *...most sweet, above all* and *...it filled my soul with exceedingly great joy.* The fruit was so desirable that he wanted more than anything else for his family to partake of it. Nephi said it was *...most desirable above all things ...most joyous to the soul.* There probably are not any better words in the English language to describe this total acceptance, love and tenderness.

We began conversing, but not with words. Communication was total and absolute and seemed to be pure thoughts communicated from mind to mind. There was no possibility of misunderstanding.

They had come to meet me and escort me to the spirit world—if I chose to go. They told me that I had a choice. I could stay or go. They did not try at all to persuade me one way or the other, but they expressed concern for Crystal and the kids if I decided not to return.

Carol was not jealous of Crystal at all. There was not the least bit of pettiness, envy or resentment. In fact, she stated that she was pleased that we had been sealed in the temple and was very concerned for Crystal's well-being if I left.

I was overjoyed to see her and bask in her love and warmth and was not eager to be separated again. She told me not to worry about our separation, that time was not the same in the spirit world. She said life was very short, that I should return and complete my responsibilities to Crystal and the children, and then we would be together again.

Granddad had white hair but appeared to be in his early forties. Mom was in her late twenties or early thirties like I remembered her when I was very young. Carol was as I remembered her in her middle to late twenties. She had brown hair. All of them wore loose-fitting, white robes. Mom's and Carol's robes were the same basic design, though slightly different.

When I emerged out of the darkness and was met by Carol, Mom, and Granddad, I noticed that we were at the scene of the accident, standing in the air above the ground about ceiling height. I could see Art sawing the tree to get the weight off of me. Then I saw him check for pulse and respiration. He thought I was dead and ran to get Mike who was working about a half-mile away. This, however, was not the focus of my attention. I was much more involved in the sweet reunion with loved ones and not concerned with what was going on below.

I remember expressing concern over being crippled. I knew what I had felt when the tree hit me, and I could see my body underneath the tree. I did not want to have the test of a handicap for the rest of my life. I felt that was probably one test I couldn't handle. They knew my thoughts and told me that if I chose to return, my body would be okay. I then agreed to go back if my body would recover. I don't remember any farewells or goodbyes. The next thing I remember I was back in my body. I immediately wiggled my toes and fingers to make sure I was not paralyzed. It hurt so badly, though, that I didn't try to do it again.

Mike and Crystal have told me things I said by the tree and at the hospital that I can't remember. It makes me think that more went on than I recall. I know I can't be sure where certain impressions came from. When Art and Mike returned, the first thing I said was that I needed to sell the motorcycle or Aaron, my oldest son, was going to kill himself on it. This thought had not occurred to me before. In fact, I had just fixed it to get it in good shape.

Mike was a trained Emergency Medical Technician and made sure I didn't try to move until he checked me out thoroughly. While he was doing that, he asked me if I had been in communication with Carol, Mom and Granddad. I said I had, but I wanted to know why he had asked. He explained that when he came to the scene, he had felt their presence. I thought it peculiar that he would mention all three.

Mike and Art spent another hour clearing a space in the trees and brush for the pickup so I could be loaded and taken to the hospital. While they were doing that, I was fading in and out of consciousness. I did not think about what had happened to me. I was just trying to cope with the pain and hang on. It wasn't until the last day in the hospital and the first few days at home that I was able to recall my out-of-body experience and try to sort things out.

When I arrived at the hospital, they were immediately concerned about internal injuries. They found that my shoulder blade was broken into six pieces, my hip had been out of socket, and I had broken one of the small bones that proceeds laterally from the vertebrae. My back felt like jelly. I guessed it was probably like deer meat that has been shot.

The doctors couldn't imagine why the force of the tree trunk, which was great enough to shatter my shoulder blade, had not crushed by back and ribs. They were also surprised that the sharpened, jagged base of the tree had not broken any skin. My clothes were torn slightly, but there was no blood anywhere.

As I had time to think about what happened, more details became clear to me. I've felt what it is to feel and enjoy the love of God. I learned that the other side is organized by families. Those people who live worthy are patriarchs and matriarchs over their families. I also received the strong impression that positions at work, in society and in the church are not important at all. What matters is how we treat people, whether or not we are kind to them and what kind of relationships we build with our families. Church positions are good because we can use them to help people, but the position itself means nothing.

All of these things were conveyed to me when a falling tree enabled me to pass beyond the veil.

CHAPTER TWO

I Could Hear Friends Calling Me Back

by Mary Bohman

During the early stages of my second pregnancy in the spring of 1982, I had a very intense dream which I still do not fully understand. I was seated at a table with a group of people and everyone's attention focused on a necklace I was wearing. I opened the locket and read the following, "Rest to appeal pardon."

I don't know what the inscription meant, other than it probably had something to do with the death of our first child whom I found strangled, at seven months, his head caught between the bars of his crib. The emotional trauma and guilt associated with that tragedy have lingered for many years, and somehow this new dream opened old wounds. At the same time it left me with a foreboding, almost an overwhelming conviction that something was going to go wrong with my present pregnancy. I knew something was going to happen, but I didn't know what.

When I was seven months along, my husband Fred invited some people over for a Friday night dinner. When they entered our home I had a premonition that I was going to get sick; but when they coughed all through dinner, I was sure I was going to catch something. I was just recovering from Epstein-bar mononucleosis, and my resistance was low.

By Sunday night my throat was sore, and I was beginning to cough. At first I thought it was just a cold. But soon I was coughing so hard it made me wet my pants. I called my mother who was a medical doctor in Richfield, Utah, at the time. The next day my father drove me from Provo to Richfield where mother could keep an eye on me.

When the coughing continued to worsen, she put me in the hospital for observation, x-rays and tests. She thought I had pneumonia, but wasn't sure. When my condition worsened, I was sent by ambulance to the hospital in Provo, where I was left to myself for three-and-a-half hours on a table in the emergency room. By now the coughing was so bad it caused me to go into labor.

They finally put me in the intensive care unit. The nurses thought I was awful because I kept ripping off the oxygen masks. I felt like I was being strangled. Between coughing seizures I just couldn't get enough air, even with the oxygen masks on. I was suffocating. The lack of oxygen in my blood was causing my heart to beat faster and faster.

They finally determined that I had the 1918 flu, a rare virus that killed millions in Europe and over 500,000 in the first six months it entered the United States. It takes a long time to diagnose because the culture normally needs about nine days to develop. Many victims are dead by then.

By the time they decided to put me on the respiratory machine, I was delirious. I remember fighting them as they pushed the first two tubes down my nose and throat. I kicked one therapist in the groin. There were seven people gathered around my bed holding me down. One man's job was just to hold my jaw still. I was afraid to die. I was fighting for my life. I was filled with a panicky, sick feeling, knowing I was slipping away, but I could do nothing about it.

Because of my struggling, I suppose, one of the tubes punctured my best lung, and it collapsed. There was blood everywhere. One of the doctors called my husband to tell him they didn't think I was going to make it.

The next thing I remember I was in a tunnel. In the distance I could hear my husband giving me a blessing. Then I could hear some other people telling me they loved me and wanted me to get well. They told me to not give up and to come back.

I realized I was gone from my body and they were calling me back. I was filled with loving feelings. The pain was gone. I didn't want to go back.

Later they told me that during this period, my eyes were rolled back and glazed over like I was dead, though my heart was still beating. My condition continued like that for hours, neither worsening or improving. Eventually everyone went home.

At about 2:30 a.m. the next morning, all my vital signs ceased. The machines reading my vital signs had zero readings. The doctors began applying electric shock in an effort to get my heart beating again.

I don't remember leaving my body at this time, but I do know something like that happened. Eventually the electric shocks got my heart beating again, and I began a long, slow, painful recovery.

I know something happened during the period when my heart was not beating, because as I began to recover I became aware that I had changed dramatically. One of the first things I noticed, while still in intensive care, was that I had lost all fear of death. If my time came, I was no longer afraid to go. I couldn't help wondering what had happened to take away that fear so completely.

The second, and probably more important thing I noticed, was that the negative, critical feelings that had dominated so much of my former thinking and feelings were suddenly gone. So were the guilt feelings associated with the death of my first child.

Two weeks after the electric shock treatment, my second child was delivered c-section, a healthy boy whom we named Ian. As I continued to mend, I noticed other changes. When I arrived home from the hospital I was a neater person. I was better able to focus my attention on important things and better able to avoid trivialities. I was happier with small things like colors as we remodeled our house and found myself taking more time to enjoy moments.

I know something happened to me during the time my body was dead and they were applying the electric shock to bring me back. I don't know why I can't remember. Maybe someday I will. All I know for sure is that something happened during that moment of forgetfulness that has changed my life.

Chapter Three

While everyone else was in Sunday School, I went to the spirit world

by Peter E. Johnson

I was called on a mission to the southern states in the spring of 1898. Soon afterwards I received a letter saying Elders Francis M. Lyman and John W. Taylor would attend the Emery Stake conference to be held the latter part of April that same year in Castle Dale, Utah, and was asked to appear before them in relation to that mission. I was set apart by Elder Heber J. Grant, of the Council of Twelve Apostles in June.

I reached Mississippi on June 22, 1898, and on August 8 was taken down with the chills and fever, which turned out to be malaria. I became so low that the president sent his counselor and two elders to see me in relation to being released and sent home. Because of a yellow fever quarantine in the area I was not allowed to leave. I was lying on a bed, burning up with fever, and the elders who had been sent to ascertain my condition were very much alarmed. They stepped out of the room and held whispered consultations. They were so far away that under ordinary circumstances I could not have heard what they said, but in some manner my hearing was made so keen that I heard their conversations as well as if they had been at my bedside. They said it was impossible to think of my recovery, and I never would go home unless I went home in a box. They decided to notify the president.

The following day I asked to be removed into the hall, where it was cooler. I was lying on a pallet, or bed. There was an attendant with me, the others having gone to Sunday School, which was being held about 100 yards away. Soon after they left I was apparently in a dying condition, and my attendant became so fearful of my appearance and condition that he left me. I desired a drink of water, but was unable to get it myself. I became discouraged and wondered why it was that I was sent to Mississippi (I had wanted to go to Kentucky where a friend was serving). I thought of my people at home and of the conditions surrounding me, and decided that I might just as well pass from this life.

Just as I reached that conclusion, this thought came to me, "You will not die unless you choose death." This was a new thought to me, and I hesitated in considering the question, then made the choice that I would rather die. Soon after that my spirit left my body, just how I cannot tell. But I perceived myself standing some four or five feet in the air, and saw my body lying lifeless on the bed. While I was in this new environment it did not seem strange, for I realized everything that was going on, and perceived that I was the same in the spirit as I had been in the body. While contemplating this new condition, something attracted my attention, and on turning around I beheld a personage who said, "You did not know I was here."

"No. But I see you are," I said. "Who are you?"

"I am your guardian angel. I have been following you constantly while on earth."

"What will you do now?" I asked.

"I am to report your presence, and you will remain here until I return."

He informed me on returning that we should wait there as my sister desired to see me, but was busy at that time. Presently she came. She was glad to see me, and asked if I was offended because she kept me waiting. She explained that she was doing some work that she wished to finish. Just before my elder sister died, she had asked me to enter into an agreement that if she died first she would watch over me, protect me from those who might seek my downfall, and that she would be the first to meet me after death. If I happened to die first, she wished me to do the same for her. We made this agreement and this was the reason that she was the first one of my relatives to meet me. After her arrival, my mother and other sisters and friends came to see me, and we discussed various topics, as we would do here on meeting friends.

After we had spent some little time in conversation, the guide came to me with a message, that I was wanted by some of the apostles who had lived on the earth during this dispensation. As soon as I came into their presence, I was asked if I desired to remain there. This seemed strange for it had never occurred to me that we would have any choice in the spirit world, as to whether we should remain there or return to earth life. I was asked if I felt satisfied with conditions there. I informed them that I was and had no desire to return to the misery and fever from which I had been suffering while in the body. After some little conversation the same question was repeated, with the same answer. Then I asked, "If I remain, what will I be asked to do?" I was informed that I would preach the gospel to the spirits there, as I had been preaching it to the people here, and that I would do so under the immediate direction of the prophet Joseph Smith. This remark brought to my mind a question which has been much discussed here, as to whether or not the prophet Joseph is now a resurrected being. While I did not verbally ask the question, they read it in my mind, and immediately said, "You wish to know whether the prophet has a body or not?"

"Yes, I would like to know," I replied.

I was told that the prophet Joseph has his body, as also his brother Hyrum, and that as soon as I could do more with my body than I could without it, my body would be resurrected.

I was again asked if I still desired to remain. This bothered me considerably, for I had already expressed myself as being satisfied. I then inquired why it was that I was asked so often if I was satisfied and if I desired to remain. I was informed that my progenitors had made a request that if I chose I might be granted the privilege of returning, to again take up my mortal body, in order that I might gather my father's genealogy and do the necessary work in the temple for my ancestors. As I was still undecided, one of the apostles said,

"We will now show you what will take place if you remain here in the spirit world, after which you can decide what to do."

We returned to the place where my body was lying. I was informed with emphasis that my first duty would be to watch the body until after it had been disposed of, as that was necessary knowledge for me to have in the resurrection.

I then saw the elders send a message to President Rich at Chattanooga, and in due time all preparations were made for the shipment of my body to Utah.

One thing seemed peculiar to me, that I was able to read the telegram as it ran along the wires, as easily as I could read the pages of a book. I could see President Rich when he received the telegram in Chattanooga. He walked the floor, wringing his hands with the thought in his mind, "How can I send a message to his father?"

The message was finally sent, and I could follow it on the wire. I saw the station and the telegraph operator at Price, Utah. I heard the instrument click as the message was received, and saw the operator write out the message and send it by phone from Price to Huntington. I also saw clearly the Huntington office and the man who received the message. I could see clearly and distinctly the people on the street. I did not have to hear what was said, for I was able to read their thoughts from their countenances.

The message was delivered to my aunt who went out with others to find my father. In due time he received the message. He did not seem overcome by the news, but began to make preparations to meet the body.

I then saw my father at the railroad station in Price, waiting for my body to arrive. Apparently he was unaffected, but when he heard the whistle of the train which was carrying my body, he went behind the depot and cried as if his heart would break.

While I was accompanying the body on the way home, I was still able to see what was going on at home. The distance, apparently, did not affect my vision. As the train approached the station, I went to my father's side, and seeing his great anguish, I informed my spirit companion that I would return to my body. He expressed his approval of my decision and said he was pleased of the choice I had made.

By some spiritual power all these things had been shown to me as they would occur if I did not return to the body. Immediately upon making this choice or decision, my companion said,

"Good, your progenitors will be pleased with your decision."

I asked why, and was told that it was their desire that I should return to the body, hunt up my father's genealogy and do their work in the temple.

During the entire visit, no one ever touched me or offered to shake my hand.

While I was in the spirit world I observed that the people there were busy and that they were perfectly organized for the work they were doing. It seemed to me a continuation of the work we are doing here. There was nothing there that seemed particularly strange to me, everything being natural.

Just how my spirit re-entered the body I cannot tell, but I saw Apostle Rich place his hands on the head of my prostrate body, and almost immediately I realized that the change had come, and I was again in the body.

The first thing that I knew was I felt a warm life-giving spot on the crown of my head, which passed through my entire body, going out to the tips of my fingers and toes. I also heard distinctly the same words that had been pronounced by Elder Grant when I was set apart for my mission,

"Go in peace, and return in safety."

After entering the body, I saw no more of the messengers who had been accompanying me, but I had a vivid recollection of all that had taken place.

The local elder who had been left to attend me, but who became frightened at my condition and went away, had not yet returned, but I later learned that he had gone to Sunday school and at the close of the services he notified them of my death.

The saints, elders and friends were gathered outside the paling, or fence, discussing the matter, and trying to decide what to do. I was still very thirsty and arose to get a drink, but found that the water was warm. I got off the pallet or bed, on which I had been lying, carried the bucket of water to the edge of the gallery, threw out the warm water, went to the well which was 75 feet deep, drew a fresh bucket of water and quenched my thirst.

The saints, elders and friends who were out at the fence, were observing all this, but feared to come near me. Finally, Brother Morton at whose house I was stopping came through the gate up the walk, towards me, but before reaching me, he turned icy cold and stopped.

I went up to him, took his hand and invited them all to come in and handle me, telling them that a spirit did not have flesh and bones as they saw me have. Brother Morton looked at me, felt of me, turned me around and then came back and handled me again, and said,

"I never was so scared in my life, for I thought you were a spirit." I told him that I was not now a spirit, but a real, tangible person.

"How could you carry that bucket of water," he asked, "throw it out and draw another, when for over a month you have been waited upon, and finally we all thought you were dead?"

I told him I had been made well, and had come back to stay with them.

A new thought came to mind. While in the spirit land, I did not shake hands with anyone, neither did anyone offer to shake hands with me, but now I felt a desire to shake hands with everyone. Then it occurred to me that the spirits of the righteous do not deceive, therefore no hand shaking. Since they don't have bodies there would be no hand to feel, although they are as pleased to meet their friends in the spirit world as they are here.

President Thomas R. Condie of the conference (district or zone) was notified of my recovery, and wrote a letter to me in which he stated,

"Ever since I consented to your release I have had no peace on that matter. Before you came to the conference the superintendent was to be released. We had no one to take his place and so I called a special fast of three days with the elders and prayed to the Lord to send someone who could take the place of Elder Dye who was soon to return home. In answer to our fasting and prayer you were sent to the conference. We became weak in the faith and asked for your release, even after we had fasted and prayed and asked the Lord to send someone here for that purpose. If agreeable, Brother Johnson, while you have been released honorably and can go home if you choose, we would like very much for you to remain here and accept the call for which the Lord has sent you into this conference."

I have often been asked how long I was in the spirit world. The last thing I remember before my departure was the singing when Sunday school commenced, and when I got up and drew the water, Sunday school had closed. The local elder did not notify them until just as they were closing. Sunday schools were held one and a half hours.

Condensed from *The Relief Society Magazine*, vol. 7, 1920, pp. 449-455.

CHAPTER FOUR

The Book Prepared Us For Tragedy

by Jill Heasley

For our fourteenth wedding anniversary, December 20, 1988, I gave my husband *Beyond the Veil,* Volume I. Before wrapping the gift I had time to read it. So did my twelve-year-old son. We were both very touched by it. I will never view life—and death—quite the same again.

When I finally gave the book to my husband Bill he seemed anxious to read it. He stayed up until 2 a.m. one morning reading the book. He said he couldn't put it down. I had gone to sleep about 10 p.m.

The next morning, Bill seemed very disturbed, like he wanted to tell me something. When I asked him what was wrong, he kept telling me he was afraid of upsetting me. Finally, after much pleading on my part, he told me what had happened.

While reading the book, he had a strong feeling of doom. He felt certain his life would be threatened. He had an overwhelming feeling that his life was in great danger. He said he was afraid of leaving me a widow and not being able to raise his four sons.

He had been right about me. I was upset, very much so. But I also felt that perhaps he was overtaken by the emotion of the book and hoped that was the only cause of his feelings.

Still, Bill felt it was more than that, so he took out a second life insurance policy. Christmas came a few days later, and we wondered if this was to be our last Christmas together.

On January 17, while Bill was preparing to close his Fresno, California, store for the day, he was shot 12 times by an armed robber. The assailant fired at least 30 shots at Bill, but only 12 had hit the target. One hit him in the stomach, going through the kidney and liver and out his back, missing the spine by one inch. The other eleven rounds lodged in his legs and ankle. He stayed conscious all the time he was being shot and watched the bullets hit him.

As the assailant fled, Bill managed to call 911 for help. The paramedics said he would have died had they arrived just a few minutes later. As it was, Bill was in intensive care for five days, and in the hospital for almost three-and-a-half weeks. We feel certain, as does everyone else involved, including doctors and police, that Bill was being carefully protected during the shooting.

Exactly a month after the shooting Bill was able to return to his store and view the damages. He found a number of bullet holes in the wall behind where he was standing the night of the shooting. These bullets had been intended for his chest and head.

Miraculously, Bill survived, and as I write this story, the doctors are expecting a full recovery with the possible exception of a permanent limp.

When the paramedics called with the news that Bill had been shot, I felt I was partly prepared, having read *Beyond the Veil.* For some reason I can't put into words, the book gave me tremendous comfort through all this.

CHAPTER FIVE

My Heart Kept Stopping

by Robert Ashford

I woke up in the middle of the night, my bed wet with sweat. I felt terrible—hot, cold, sweaty, and sick to my stomach. I got up. The alarm clock said 2 a.m. I went outside for a breath of fresh air.

I sat on the patio for a while, finally beginning to feel better. It was a hot, muggy night. East Texas is known for its hot, sticky weather in the summer.

Before I returned to bed I turned the thermostat from 76 to 72. My wife Sonja didn't like it that cool, but she was asleep and I was awake. The clock said 3:35 a.m. as I rolled back into bed. I needed to get some sleep as it would be daylight soon and time to go to work.

At about 11 a.m. I still wasn't feeling well. Our company was involved in wiring two schools, and the work wasn't going well. It was time for me to leave the office for one of the work sites in Winnsboro, about two hours away. The drive is somewhat tricky, especially the short route.

I stopped about two miles north of Gilmore, got out of the car and walked into the woods. I felt terrible. At the time I'm not sure why I walked into the woods. I just did. I found a stump and sat down.

August in east Texas can be hell. The humidity that day was about 95 percent and the temperature at least 98 degrees. I felt like all the strength had left my body. I began looking for a place to lie down. I'm not sure how long I was there, but with each passing moment I felt worse.

I was worried about conditions at work. Lone Star Steel, our biggest account, had shut down. We were having labor overruns and lost productivity on several of our largest jobs.

My son Wes had just returned home from his mission. He was 30 pounds underweight and very ill. The doctors were concerned about him but couldn't identify his physical problem. Our oldest daughter was having serious marriage problems.

As I sat there in the woods, alone, pondering my problems, I began to pray for help. I asked that whatever was needed in my life to help solve the problems would happen. I pleaded for help.

It was about 7 p.m. when I pulled into the driveway that night. The longer the day went on, the worse I seemed to feel. I'd been suffering with headaches for several months. I was taking medication at regular intervals to keep them tolerable. Dinner was ready, but I couldn't eat. I went to bed early.

I woke up very early the next morning from what seemed to be a dream. I was lying in bed looking at my feet. The problem was they were a couple of feet above the bed. I could see them and my legs rising into the air but I was still in the bed. I fought to wake up. It was a struggle. My whole body wanted to float into the air. I began screaming and fighting to remain in bed—feeling that if I left I would never return. Finally I won the battle. My body felt normal again.

I laid there for the longest time, exhausted. I was wet with sweat. It was 4 a.m. and I couldn't go back to sleep. I got up, showered, shaved and got ready for work. It was 5 a.m. when I arrived at the office and began working on an estimate.

Other employees began arriving between 6:30 and 7:00 a.m. My office door was open. Most of them stopped in to say good morning. About 7 a.m. my secretary arrived. She came into my office and asked if I needed anything. I told her I wasn't feeling well and was going home for awhile. I left at 7:15 a.m.

Instead of going home I drove to the hospital. After parking and locking the car I entered the emergency room door. The nurse in charge looked at me and knew I was in trouble. She called for help, and before I knew it, I was on a table with an EKG monitor hooked to my chest and extremities. A doctor was giving directions like a traffic cop at a busy intersection, all the time asking me questions. By now my headache was beating like a base drum in time with my heart beat. They gave me a shot that made me sweat and feel light-headed. I began to feel better. The doctor seemed relieved. He left for a few minutes. When he returned, I was asleep.

After waking up I remember lying there looking at the EKG monitor. All of a sudden the line went straight. The beep became constant. The next thing I remember a nurse was waking me up by shaking my shoulder. The doctor came in and gave me two small pills. My head began to ache again. The next thing I remember I was going through the hospital halls to the elevator, then into the intensive care unit (ICU).

They hooked me up to several machines and stuck a tube in my arm and began to pump me full of fluid. A nurse stayed with me for a long time, regularly taking my blood pressure and listening to my chest. I wondered if she was listening to see when I was full so they could take the "hose" out of my arm.

I looked at the nurse and asked her what her name was. She asked me how I felt. I looked directly into her eyes and said,

"I'm leaving now."

"Where are you going?" she asked. Then I was gone. I don't remember how long, but the medical report said 30 seconds.

When I awakened the nurse was beating on my chest. I had an oxygen mask on. She saw me open my eyes. She looked at me and said,

"Don't go away again, O.K.?"

A few seconds later the room was full of doctors and nurses. I received another shot and they began checking me over with great intensity. They called my wife, and in what seemed a very short time, she was at my side. They talked to her in private, just out of range of my hearing. It seemed very serious.

My chest began to hurt. The longer I laid there, the more it hurt. I remember thinking how strong that nurse was, the one who had pounded on my chest.

It was late now and dark outside. Sonja left for home, and the nurses were getting the patients ready for the night. They gave me another shot. The "hose" in my arm hurt worse than my chest.

Early the next morning, before sunrise, .my room was suddenly full of nurses again. Lights were flashing, and that beep began again. I saw the face of the nurse from the main desk. She was 30 or 40 feet away looking at the monitor.

The next thing I remember I was waking up. Again, a nurse was pounding on my chest. A doctor came in and ordered another shot. I felt confused. I wished they would quit hitting me. My chest hurt more than ever.

Sonja and Wes came in, and so did a specialist. They all seemed very concerned. When they finally got around to talking to me, the doctor said I needed a pacemaker implant to keep my heart going, and he wanted to put it in that afternoon. I agreed to go ahead with it. The doctor warned me, however, that the pacemaker was probably just a temporary solution. More analysis and possibly surgery would be necessary.

In preparing for surgery the nurse shaved my chest and gave me a sedative. I became very tired and dozed off to sleep. Suddenly, I was not in the hospital anymore.

I was in a large, white room. It was beautiful. The floor was amber gold, and it reflected every image like a mirror. The walls were trimmed in gold. At one end of the room stood two large doors, also trimmed in gold.

I wasn't in the room alone. There were three other people. I was standing on my feet, feeling glorious. The others were looking at me since I had just arrived.

As I looked at the only woman in the room, something amazing happened. I could read her personality. Not a word was spoken, but I could instantly tell the character of her very being. She was a prostitute.

Then I looked at the two men. One was tall and blond. He was a salesman. The other was a short, dark-haired businessman. I was amazed at my understanding of these people.

I stood there waiting, but I didn't know for what. Then the two large doors opened, filling the room with an even brighter, almost blinding light. A man came through the open doors. He was dressed in white and came towards me. The closer he got the more love I felt. When he stood before me, my whole being was filled with the love he had for me.

This magnificent being stood before me, and without verbally speaking, asked me why I wanted to live. The question caused great reflection. I thought about all the problems I'd been facing—work, Wes's health, my daughter's marriage. It seemed I had a greater burden than I was capable of enduring. I was tempted to tell the man I didn't want to go on living, but I hesitated.

I dearly loved my wife. It wouldn't be fair to leave her alone with all the problems and two young girls still to raise. I realized my oldest daughter would need me more now than ever before. My son needed my love and encouragement. I also realized how much I loved the Lord. I wanted desperately to serve him. I wanted for him to find confidence in me enough to let me love and serve him the remainder of my life.

The man in white looked at me, and without uttering a word, told me they would let me know what the decision was.

"Mr. Ashford, Mr. Ashford. Are you with us again?" cried a female voice.

I opened my eyes and saw a nurse standing over me. I looked around the room. There were two nurses and a doctor administering to me again. I received another injection, and they stayed with me until it was time to leave for surgery. I later found out my heart had stopped for one minute and 45 seconds.

Sonja, Wes and Rick Johnson, our home teacher, came in before I left for surgery. They gave me a priesthood blessing. I was very groggy and didn't understand much of what was said in the blessing.

After the surgery I felt terrible. My chest hurt. I was sick to my stomach. I felt horrible.

Sonja was there, and stayed by me for a couple of hours. When I began coming around, it was twilight. Sonja and I were talking. I began to tell her what had happened. She listened intently.

Then all of a sudden my chest was filled with excruciating pain, and I passed out. When I woke up the room was full of doctors and nurses again. Sonja was gone. I didn't know what had happened. The doctor told me I would have to return to surgery. The pacemaker was not functioning properly.

Sonja and Wes returned. They asked me to talk some more about the white room. I told them everything up to the part about their letting me know whether or not I would be allowed to continue living. Sonja asked if I knew what the decision was. I replied that we would soon know because I was going back into surgery.

The next thing I remember I was in the operating room. I could hear the doctors talking. They were arguing about how the pacemaker was wired. I became angry and turned to the anesthesiologist. I told him I was an electrician, and if they needed help I could fix the wires.

The anesthesiologist was a friend of mine. We went to the same LDS ward. He looked at me and said I was going to be OK, that I was going to live. I knew he was speaking the truth. I had my answer. I went to sleep.

The next morning the surgeon came in and explained what had happened to the pacemaker. He said he had made a mistake, connecting the wires backwards. He apologized for the problem. I appreciated his honesty.

Five days later I was released from the hospital, ready to continue my life.

Chapter Six

An End to Bitterness

by Ethel Winn Cole Kilts

I worked as an ordinance worker in the Ogden Temple for several years. On one occasion I was acting as the first follower on a session. As I was sitting on the stand in the chapel watching the patrons as they came in, I noticed a lovely older lady with a young man. I supposed he was probably her son, maybe there to get his endowments for a mission. I noticed them several times as the room was filling.

As we moved on to the endowment room and all were seated, this sweet lady was on the front row, just a few seats away from me. Not long after the session started, I had the most beautiful feeling come over me, so peaceful, penetrating so deep with a complete love, joy and happiness. The tears rolled down my cheeks. I carefully tried to wipe them away without drawing attention to me. I knew we had a heavenly visitor with us. I could perceive that it was male. I couldn't see him or hear his voice. I could just feel his unmistakable presence.

"Could it be my father with a message for me?" I asked myself. No, I could sense that it was a young person. The feelings I felt are indescribable, feelings you want to keep with you always. Soon it was time to leave the room and finish the session.

After my duties were through, I started down the escalator to the main floor. As I reached the bottom, the dear, sweet lady had just come from the dressing room and was ready to leave the temple. She stopped me and asked if she could speak to me.

She asked if I had felt anything different in the endowment room. The tears came quickly to my eyes as I told her I had. I told her I had distinctly felt the presence of a young man.

She said she had too and that it was her son who had recently been killed in a bicycle accident on his mission in the Washington D.C. area. The young man with her had been her son's companion at the time of the accident.

She said she couldn't understand why her son had to be taken while on his assignment for the Lord. She said she felt anger and frustration. The mission president had talked to her and tried to convince her that her son had just gone from one mission assignment to a greater one. She said that had helped for a while, but soon she was back to frustration and anger. She had received several blessings, but they hadn't helped. The bitterness was too deep.

We shed many tears together as she told of her hurt. Then she said her son had impressed on her during the temple session that she should not mourn any more, but know that he was busy teaching the gospel to many who have been waiting for years.

"I am happier than I have ever been," he had communicated to her, his spirit to hers. "Please, Mother, be happy for me."

I left the temple that night realizing I had just experienced one of the most glorious days of my life, a sacred, beautiful day to be remembered always.

CHAPTER SEVEN

The Old Black Ledger Book

by Harriett Anthony

I grew up in southwestern Massachusetts following World War II. Our family lived in a small, rented home in the then rural town of Southwick. Our nearest neighbor, directly across the road, was one of the old New England farm families. The Hastings had many acres of farm ground, an imposing barn, and a small one-and-a-half story Cape Cod home at least 200 years old.

Our families were close and shared many happy times together. But all too soon we moved. I grew up. The Hastings farm was sold by a surviving son, and little now remains.

In the transition, my father maintained possession of an old scrapbook, or perhaps a ledger, from our friends, the Hastings. It fell into my possession upon my father's death. It is a quaint, black folio, filled with farming clippings cut from now long-gone newspapers, pages and pages of hand written accounts, and all sorts of other odd items. I kept it mostly as a curiosity. It wasn't until years later that I realized its true importance.

In 1981 my husband, son and I joined the Church of Jesus Christ of Latter-day Saints, later being endowed and sealed in the Washington D.C. Temple. It soon became apparent that my one true gift and calling was genealogical and temple work. I received callings to work in the ward and stake genealogical libraries. My husband was a veil worker; and wherever I put my hand in the work of the dead, it seemed to find success.

Then one day I turned my thoughts to those fine, hard working, Massachusetts farmers, the Hastings, who had so enriched my childhood. I sent a letter to the town clerk of Southwick, asking for information on "Francsis Hasteings." To my surprise, and sorrow, they had no record.

That seemed to be the end of the matter. My usual Midas touch for genealogy had failed me.

Then one night my mind was opened to a dream, that I am now convinced was a vision. I am as sure of that as I am of the sun coming up in the morning.

I saw the home that had belonged to the Hastings, just as I knew it as a child. But there was one difference. The front of the house had not one, but two front doors. In the doorway to the left stood a woman, wearing a long, white dress.

As I neared the door she asked,

"Do you remember this house?"

"Yes, but why are there two doors?" I replied.

"The family is apart and only you can unite them again," she explained. "Remember, the name is spelled *Hastings,* not Hasteings." The vision then faded, and I awoke, but the memory of it remained.

The next day I looked through the old black ledger, looking perhaps for clues, just what I was not sure. In the course of the search, on an old yellow ledger page, at the end of a long inventory, was the name Frederick Hastings.

All my genealogical instincts were telling me to follow this lead. In short order I wrote a second letter, this time asking for information on Frederick Hastings.

At the end of several very long weeks, the reply came. The town clerk had the records for Frederick, his six brothers and sisters, with dates and places and even information on the father, Francsis, born in 1836.

There was enough and more to send the names to the church genealogical department in Utah for approval to do temple ordinances. It took six long months before the permission finally arrived.

Some young people did the baptisms. I was able to act as proxy in the endowments and sealings for the women of the family, and a temple worker was proxy for all the males. At the temple, and later at home, I felt a debt had been paid, kindness returned. I turned my attention to other matters.

About two weeks after the temple work was completed I had another dream or vision. I felt like Paul in the New Testament when he said he could not tell if he was in or out of his body.

I stood again in the fields of the old Hastings farm. Again the house came into view—the same again, yet different. This time there was only one door, and if it could ever be said that a house could be happy, this home radiated what seemed to be the essence of happiness.

I approached the remaining door, and it opened all by itself. Inside the house were the Hastings family members, in high spirits and celebrating. One spoke to me and said,

"You have brought us together, and given us much joy. Come in and visit."

I entered, and was roundly greeted by all. The interior of the house was as new and bright as it was

200 years ago. I noted on a table a small, clear stone. My host noticed that it caught my attention. He asked me if I wanted it, to which I replied that I did. They all pressed the gift upon me, and as I reached to touch it, I found myself back in my own house and in bed.

The matter of the stone has puzzled me. My husband believes it is a seer stone, which the scriptures say all the faithful will have. Only time will tell if that is the right answer.

I do know that my skill and good fortune as a genealogist has continued to increase—finding long lost ancestors, missing wives, lost dates and all the other obstacles that beset a genealogist are as April snow before a noontime sun. I often feel the presence and help of deceased members of the Hastings family.

For some, life beyond the veil may be an intellectual abstraction, or perhaps a religious abstraction. For me the conviction has gone beyond mere faith. It is real.

CHAPTER EIGHT

Uncle Hance Wore Gum Boots

by LeRoi C. Snow

Editor's note:

"The dead shall rise and come forth at thy bidding," was the promise made to Lorenzo Snow, when he was a young man twenty-two years of age, by the first patriarch of the LDS church, Joseph Smith Sr. The following experience was recorded by his son, LeRoi C. Snow.

For several weeks twenty-year-old Ella Jensen had lingered between life and death with scarlet fever. On one particular night, a close girl friend, Lea

Reese, was staying with her to relieve Ella's over-weary parents of the night vigil.

"About three o'clock in the morning," she relates, "I was suddenly awakened by Ella calling me. She was excited. She said, " 'They are coming to get me at ten o'clock in the morning. I am going to die, and they are coming at ten o'clock to take me away. I must get ready. Will you help me?'

"She asked me to call her parents. I explained to her that they were tired and asleep and it would be better not to disturb them.

" 'You must call them,' she said. 'I want to tell them now.' "

The parents were called, and she explained that her Uncle Hance, who was dead, had appeared to her while she was awake, her eyes open, and told her that the messengers were to be there at ten o'clock to conduct her into the spirit world. The parents thought that she was delirious and tried to get her to quiet down and go to sleep, but she insisted that she was going to die and that they were coming for her. She wanted to see the members of the family and bid them goodby.

As ten o'clock approached, Ella's father, who was holding her hand, felt the pulse become very weak. A few moments later it stopped; he turned to his wife and said, "She has gone; her pulse has stopped." The grief-stricken parents concluded to send for President Lorenzo Snow, the girl's uncle, and advise him.

President Snow, upon receiving the word, left a meeting in the tabernacle and invited Rudger Clawson, who was then president of the Box Elder stake, to accompany him to the Jensen home. President Snow was Brother Jensen's brother-in-law. When they arrived at the home they found the family almost hysterical with grief.

President Clawson relates: "As we entered the home, we met Sister Jensen who was very much alarmed. We went to Ella's bedside. We were impressed by the thought that her spirit had passed out of the body and gone beyond. Turning to me, President Snow said, 'Brother Clawson will you anoint her?' which I did. We then laid our hands upon her head and the anointing was confirmed by President Snow. He blessed her, and among other things, used this very extraordinary expression in a commanding voice, 'Come back, Ella, come back. Your work upon the earth is not completed. Come back.' Shortly thereafter, we left the home. President Snow said to the parents, 'Now do not mourn or grieve any more, it will be all right. Brother Clawson and I are busy and must go. We cannot stay, but you must be patient and wait, and do not mourn because it will be all right.' "

Her father said that she remained in this condition for an hour and a half after President Snow left the house. Three hours from the time she first passed away, her parents remained sitting by her bedside watching, and waiting, when all at once she opened her eyes. She looked about the room, saw her parents sitting there and still looked for someone else. First thing she said was, 'Where is he?' They asked whom she was referring to. 'Brother Snow,' she replied. 'He called me back.' They told her he had gone. She said, 'Why did he call me back? I was happy. I did not want to come back.'

Regarding the more than three-and-one-half hours that Ella spent in the spirit world, she said:

"At ten o'clock, my spirit left my body. It took me some time to make up my mind to go as I could hear and see the folks crying and mourning over me. It was very hard for me to leave them. As soon as I had a glimpse of the other world, I was anxious to go, and all the cares of the world left me.

"I entered a large hall. It was so long that I could not see the end of it, and it was filled with people. As I went through this hall, the first person I recognized was my grandpa, H.P. Jensen, who was sitting in one end of the room, writing. He looked up somewhat surprised to see me and said, 'Why, there is my granddaughter Ella.' He was very much pleased, greeted me and as he continued with his writing, I passed on through the room and met many of my relatives and friends. It was like going along the crowded streets of a city where you meet many people, only a very few of whom you recognize. People seemed to be in family groups. Some inquired about their friends and relatives on the earth. Among this number was my cousin.

"The people were all dressed in white, excepting Uncle Hance Jensen who had on his dark clothes, long rubber boots, the things he wore when he was drowned in the Snake River in Idaho.

"Everybody appeared to be perfectly happy. I was having a very pleasant visit with each one that I knew.

"When I reached the end of the long room, I opened the door and went into another room filled with children. They were all arranged in perfect order, the smallest ones first, the larger ones according to age and size in the back rows all around the room. They seemed to be convened in a sort of primary or Sunday school, presided over by Aunt Eliza R. Snow. There were hundreds of small children."

It was while she was listening to the children sing that she heard President Snow's voice. He said, "Sister Ella, you must come back as your mission is not finished here on earth."

"So I just spoke to Aunt Eliza," Ella explained, "and told her that I must go back."

She obeyed this call although it was very much against her desire, such perfect peace and happiness prevailed there. There was no suffering, no sorrow. This was always a source of comfort to her. She learned by this experience that we should not grieve too much for our departed loved ones, especially at the time they leave us.

"As I was leaving," Ella said, "the only regret I had was that the folks were grieving so much for me, but I soon forgot all about this world in my delight with the other. For more than three hours my spirit was gone from my body. As I returned, I could see my body lying on the bed and the folks gathering about in the room. I hesitated for a moment, then thought, 'Yes, I will go back for a little while.' I told the folks I would stay only a short time to comfort them."

She said there was practically no pain on leaving the body in death, but the pain was intense in coming back to life.

President Clawson writes concerning this case, "Sometime before this advent into the spirit world, Uncle Hance, who lived in Brigham City, counseled with me as President of the stake concerning the propriety of moving into Snake River country, Idaho, to engage in salmon fishing. His idea was that if he was successful, he could ship salmon from the north to Brigham City at a good profit and thus profit himself financially. He needed the help that such a business would bring him. I said that if it was his wish to get into that business, it was all-right with the stake presidency and the matter was for him to decide for himself. He left for the north and at once turned his attention to salmon fishing.

"One morning he went from the home where he was staying, clothed in a jumper and overalls with gum boots to fish, but he never returned. His oldest brother, Jacob Jensen, came to me greatly alarmed and said that no word had been received from Hance for some time, and nobody seemed to know where he was. He was greatly excited about it and feared that his brother had been drowned in the Snake River. Jacob organized a posse of men and at once instituted a search covering a period of some two or three weeks at Snake River, but their efforts were fruitless. No trace could be found of Hance, and he was never again heard from until his niece, Ella Jensen, met him in the spirit world. She said that he was dressed in a jumper and overalls with gum boots. The mystery was solved. There seemed to be no doubt thereafter that Hance Jensen was drowned in the Snake River. It is said that when the dead manifest themselves to the living, they usually appear as they were last seen on earth so that the living may recognize them. If that be true, it accounts for the strange habit that her uncle was wearing."

While in this large building in the spirit world, Ella met a woman who greeted her, said she was Aunt Mary and told her she died while Ella was a baby. Ella's mother asked if she could describe her. The answer was, "Yes, she was a tall woman with black hair, dark eyes and thin features."

"Yes," the mother answered, "Surely you have described your Aunt Mary."

"I also met another woman there," Ella continued, "who said she was my Aunt Sarah and had died before I was born."

"Will you describe her," the mother asked.

"Yes, she was rather short and somewhat fleshy, with round features, light hair and blue eyes."

"Why yes, Ella, that is your Aunt Sarah. You have described her perfectly."

"It may well be thought," Brother Clawson continues, "that Ella Jensen's work was not completed as indicated by President Snow, for she afterwards became president of the Young Ladies Mutual Improvement Association in Brigham City, and afterwards she married and became a mother in Israel. Surely a woman can do no greater work in the world than to become a mother in Israel."

Ella Jensen was born August 3, 1871. This experience occurred March 3, 1891, in her twentieth year. She married Henry Wright, March 20, 1895, and was the mother of eight children. She lived in Brigham City, Utah.

CHAPTER NINE

I Had to Cross a Great Gulf

by Nancy Lee Minter

I was a widow when I married Myrl, my second husband, in 1983. He had two beautiful teenage daughters who decided to come and live with their father and me, instead of with their mother. The oldest, Chris, was working, but Lori, the baby, was 15 at the time.

When Lori was 16, she started to work at a pizza place where she met a young man, Rick, whom she brought home for dinner. I knew he was a Mormon because he didn't drink tea, or coffee or anything like that. He always wore a white shirt. He was very different. I had come from a non-LDS background, and didn't know very much about Mormons.

When Rick started coming over, I talked to my minister about it. He told me to try to discourage this new relationship because Mormons were not Christians. By the next year, the friendship between Lori and Rick got serious.

One St. Patrick's day evening, Myrl and I went dancing. When he twirled me, I heard something snap. I started to fall forward. Something else snapped, then I started to fall backwards. I knew my leg was broken, and I crumbled to the floor.

I hurt so badly. I couldn't look down. I was taken by ambulance to an Oklahoma City hospital. The doctor said I had broken both ankle bones. He put a cast on my ankle to hold me over to Monday when surgery would be required.

The surgery took place on Monday. When I awoke on Tuesday, there were doctors all around me. There was a big machine. When I asked what was the matter, they said I had turned blue, that they thought I had had some kind of reaction to the pain killer or anesthetic I was receiving. One doctor said I had someone up there who loved me. He said I had returned from the dead, but I don't remember anything that happened while I was gone from my body. I had four more surgeries after this on my ankle.

Lori and Rick got engaged. I had continued to discuss the matter with my pastor, and he told me how immoral Mormons were, that I was not to have any contact with the church or the bishop. I didn't even know what a bishop was. He explained to me that a bishop was like a minister.

We had talked to Lori and told her we wanted them to get married in the Baptist church. Rick refused. He said he wanted a garden wedding. We finally agreed to do that, but insisted that a Mormon bishop could not perform the marriage.

Over the next few months we made life so miserable for Lori and Rick that one night we told her she was a cultist and a non-Christian. Things came to a peak. Lori moved out in the middle of the night. She was crying. I was crying. I was losing my girl.

She moved in with Rick's brother and his wife. They later drove to Utah where they were married in a garden wedding at Rick's parents' house. Afterwards they returned to Oklahoma City to live.

It was almost two years that we did not talk. Communication finally opened again when Lori became pregnant with her first child. When she was in the hospital to have the baby, Rick's mother came out from Utah. We were both at the hospital, and I felt very uncomfortable. Lori was having a very hard time with her labor.

Finally the doctor said if things didn't start happening within an hour he would have to take the baby by caesarean operation. Lori had been in labor a long time and by now was very weak.

That's when Lori's mother-in-law, Lola, said she had to call home to talk to her husband to ask him to use his priesthood authority to help. I didn't know what she was talking about. This was all very strange to me.

After calling her husband, Lola took Rick aside, saying they had to go in Lori's room in five minutes. They did and told Lori at that moment her father-in-law who was in Salt Lake was also praying for her. A half-hour later our grandchild was born.

I was amazed by all these events. After it was over I got Lola aside and asked her if the Mormons believed in Jesus Christ. She looked at me utterly amazed and said,

"What do you think the name of our church is?"

I told her I didn't know. I had only heard the name Mormon up until this time. She told me the official name was The Church of Jesus Christ of Latter-day Saints. I told her I would like to know more.

About three months later Rick and Lori invited us to the baby's blessing. My husband had to work, so it was agreed that I would go. I sat through the sacrament meeting and the blessing, then went to an investigators' class. Everything seemed very strange. I felt pulled in all directions. After that I went to Relief Society and felt very comfortable.

On the way home Rick asked what I thought about it. I said things were very foreign to me, and I needed time to think about it. The missionaries started coming over. Knowing better than to tell Myrl, I kept it a secret from him. Of what I am not sure, but I was very afraid.

I was up to the fifth or sixth lesson when Rick called to ask if I had told my husband yet that I was seeing the missionaries. I told him I hadn't. I didn't think that I should.

"Mother, you are living a lie if you don't tell him," Rick said. "Would you tell him tonight?"

I told him I would. That afternoon I prayed, and I cried. I was really afraid when Myrl walked in the door. I said I had something to tell him, and began to cry. Before I could get it out he said,

"Yes, I know," he said, "you have been studying with the missionaries, and I disapprove."

Rick and Lori came over a short time later. There was a big argument.

"Dad," Rick said, "why don't you at least take the missionary lessons and see if you like it. Pray about it and find out if it's right."

After much discussion, Myrl decided he would listen to the missionaries. When they came over we decided to start form the beginning. At first there was much animosity. Myrl argued and said he didn't believe. But with time he began to listen, and we began going to church too, attending the investigators' class.

In 1988, October 27, we were baptized. In November of that same year I was operated on for a hernia. I requested a private room but they didn't have one in the hospital. Two days later I was given pain medicine, too much. I went code blue. Something strange happened. A doctor came in a little after 10 p.m. to discuss upcoming surgery with the woman in the next bed. He looked over and noticed that I wasn't breathing.

He ordered the lady in the next bed to hit the button and yell code blue. This she did while he jumped on my bed and began giving me CPR. The same thing happened as before, my heart had stopped.

"Welcome back," said my doctor when it was all over.

"Where have I been?" I asked.

"You died," he said. "If the other doctor hadn't come in and noticed you, you wouldn't be here."

He said I was very susceptible to the drugs they had used on me. He said they would start giving me something else for the pain.

When I arrived home the Relief Society sisters began bringing over food, and helping out around the house. I was not used to this kind of thing, not even in the Baptist Church.

January 5, 1989, we moved into our new stake center so we wouldn't have to drive to Oklahoma City any more. I was the food chairman. In February we were scheduled to have a dinner for the couples in the ward. I had been having migraine headaches for several weeks, and they were getting so bad I went to the doctor.

He had given me a shot and told me to go home and go to bed, but with the dinner coming up, and the fact that we were expecting a big crowd, I told my husband I needed to be there, so he took me.

When I arrived, my head was still hurting, so I asked the bishop to give me a blessing. The bishop and another priesthood holder took me into a private room and gave me a blessing, but the pain did not go away. Soon it was so bad, I had to ask my husband to take me home.

I got as far as the door and passed out. When the ambulance arrived, I came to and insisted they take me home. One of the sisters insisted I go to the hospital, so I finally agreed to do that.

I went into the emergency room where they read my blood pressure at 280 over 120. The doctor asked if it had ever been that high before. I said "No, just give me something for my head." They decided to do some tests.

They had trouble getting blood out of my left wrist, then sent me up to get a cat scan. They gave me a form to sign, but not having my glasses, I couldn't read it, so I just signed it. The first part of the cat scan went fine.

The nurse said she was going to give me a shot that would make me feel very warm and very good. She gave me the shot. I began to feel hot, but there was something wrong. I couldn't breathe.

I began to get out from under the cat scan machine. The technician began to tell me to get back. I had enough breath to tell her I could not breathe. She ran to the red phone and started to yell, "Stat, stat, any doctor, stat, stat."

My whole body was shaking. I couldn't get any air at all. Doctors started running in. I knew I was going to die. There was no doubt about it. I was fighting it. There were still a lot of things for me to do.

I prayed to my Heavenly Father, telling him that if I had sinned, to please forgive me. Then I slipped into unconsciousness.

A few minutes later, they gave me something to counteract the iodine I had taken. It helped for a few minutes. I still believed I was going to die. There was no more fight left in me. I said, "Heavenly Father, I deliver unto thee my spirit."

When I had said this, I could see my body on the table, shaking violently. I was transported to the most beautiful place I had ever seen, so beautiful I cannot adequately describe it. I heard harps playing—and they were made of gold, so ornate, so beautiful.

The room was so bright that it hurt my eyes—at least at first. I saw men and women standing around a throne that was made of gold. I didn't see Heavenly Father sitting on the throne, but I knew it was his. I heard the most beautiful music I had ever heard.

Everyone was wearing white robes, so white as to defy description. And everyone was praising Heavenly Father with the most beautiful music I had ever heard. I don't know how long I stood there, but I had a guide at my side, someone I had known—like we had been friends for years.

There was a great gulf I had to cross in order to be where Heavenly Father was, but I couldn't cross it.

I knew that if I tried to cross it there would be no return. I just wanted to stay and hear the beautiful music and the praises to Heavenly Father.

Then, suddenly, I was transported back. I didn't want to come back, but there was something compelling me to return. Then I was standing above my body, and I could see the doctors working on me. They were swearing.

"Why is she still wearing her pants, and her shoes, and her stockings?" one asked. Things weren't going right for them. There was more cussing and swearing. One of the problems was that I still had on my garments, not the top but the bottoms. I was wearing my hospital gown. I could see my body shaking and quivering from electric shock. I wondered why they wouldn't leave me alone, why they wouldn't let me go. I finally decided there was probably still something important for me to do. This was the third time I had died, but the first time I had gone beyond the veil. Yes, there had to be a reason for me to stick around.

It was 10 p.m. when they gave me the iodine. Now it was after 2 a.m. I had come back. I was a little sad. I still had my headache, worse than ever. I was crying and really didn't want to come back.

They took me back to emergency where my husband was waiting. They talked to him first. He told me I would be spending more time in intensive care. I began to cry. I asked for something for the pain. They said they couldn't give me anything, that I just had to tough it out. For the rest of the day there was no rest. They checked me every fifteen minutes. The doctor told me I was not only allergic to iodine but some of the other things they had given me too.

I asked to go home, but the doctor said I couldn't. He finally agreed to let me go into a regular room where it might be easier to get some rest. He said it was possible for me to have a flashback reaction, and I had to be where they could treat me.

I was taken to the private room. I wasn't afraid, but knew Heavenly Father was with me. The day before I had received my patriarchal blessing that said my kindred dead were waiting for me to do their work for them, also that I would receive many trials and tests that would make me stronger.

It had seemed every time we tried to go to the temple in Dallas, Satan had tried to block our way. As soon as I got out of the hospital, my husband and I became earnestly engaged in getting our genealogies in order so the work for the dead could begin.

Chapter Ten

I Could Hear Him Singing

by Seth Boyer

The shimmering sun bore down on us, and it seemed the time to get off work would never come. My friends and I were weeding Utah sugar beets in July. The rows were a quarter mile long but seemed ten miles as the day wore on. It was back-breaking work, or so it seemed. I was eleven years old, the youngest of the boys in the field that day.

Someone threw out the idea that we go swimming down at the ponds as soon as we finished work. We all jumped on the idea, knowing how refreshing the cool water would be in the 100-degree heat. When quitting time rolled around, we all piled into a car one of the boys was driving and headed home for swim suits and tubes.

Upon arriving at the pond, I was determined to be the first in the water. In my excitement I quickly pumped up one of the tubes, and without bothering to take off my clothes, jumped into the water. Sitting on the tube I paddled out into deeper water. Not only did I have on all my work clothes but also my big work boots. The other boys were still on the bank, stripping down to underwear, or putting on swimming suits. I had succeeded in being the first in the water.

All of a sudden I was conscious of an unwanted, sickening sound—a hissing, bubbling sound. I looked down and saw my old tube was leaking and going flat fast.

I wasn't the best of swimmers but figured I could make it back to shore. The instant I jumped off the sinking tube I knew I was in deep trouble. My work boots and jeans were like lead weights pulling me down.

I yelled for help, but the boys only laughed, thinking I was joking. But when I went under, and came up gasping for air, one of the boys knew I was dead serious and jumped in to come and help.

As I was struggling desperately for my life a strange thing happened. After I had gone down for the third or fourth time, I thought I heard a voice, saying, "This is it. Give up." And so I did, and began sinking into darkness.

My life didn't flash before me, nor did I see a bright light or anything like that. I was just sinking quietly into darkness.

Then I felt arms around my waist. My friend and neighbor David Dean was pushing me up to the life-giving air. As we reached the surface I gasped to clear my airways as another boy arrived with an extra tube. Together we paddled to shore. I thanked them for their help, but never told them how close I had come to drowning.

I come from a large family of twelve children. I am number ten. Dad taught us to work. Sometimes we didn't like it, but now I know he did the right thing.

My mother was 49 when she had her last baby—a healthy, happy boy named Creed. I was five years older than he, and we had a sister, Wanda, in between. The rest of the children ranged from two to twenty years older than I.

We had a lot of fun on our Springville farm, as well as learning how to work. I have fond memories of throwing the football to little Creed on our big front lawn. I remember father trying to grow grain in front of our house, but after the kids trampled it down for a few years, he just left it in grass. I remember pushing Wanda on the large swing, and teasing little Creed, sometimes too much as big brothers sometimes do.

By the time I was twelve, the older brother I admired most at the time, had rebelled against my parents. He had taken up smoking and drinking. I admired him for his daring, reckless ways. I wanted to be like him. Sometimes he would get an old car, strap himself in it, then race into the fields to see how many times he could roll it over. Fortunately, no one was hurt, at least not seriously.

Then came the day that everything changed. It was a Friday in May, and I remember sitting in school hearing the fire truck siren. I had a strange feeling that it had something to do with me. As I walked home that afternoon I could see a lot of cars in front of the house and wondered what had happened.

Earlier in the day my younger brother Creed had come home from school—first grade—with a headache. When mother put him to bed he said,

"Mommy, I'm dying. Pray for me, Mommy. I'm dying."

She tried to comfort him, telling him he wasn't dying, then went to the kitchen to get him a drink of water. When she returned he had stopped breathing. She called the fire department. They took him to the hospital.

By Sunday evening church everyone in our ward or congregation had been praying for Creed.

When I left the meeting to get into the car, I was told he had died without ever regaining consciousness.

I was devastated and bitter. I couldn't understand how a healthy, happy little boy could just die like that. I still don't know for sure what caused the death. The doctors guessed it might have been encephalitis.

The next few days were hard as many people came to our home. I was expected to come out of my room and show my face. Then came the viewing, with all of us standing in line. All the time I felt like my heart was breaking, and the bitterness was getting worse.

At the funeral, we were all seated on one bench, from the oldest to the youngest. Next to me was my sister Wanda, who was now the youngest living. As I sat there next to her, my face was buried in my hands. I couldn't seem to bear the fact that Creed was really gone. My heart ached.

During the service, Creed's classmates from school came to the front of the chapel and sang a simple, but beautiful song, "I Am A Child of God." Some of the verses I remember are,

"I am a child of God
And he has sent me here,
Has given me an earthly home
With parents kind and dear.

Lead me, guide me, walk beside me,
Help me find the way,
Teach me all that I most do
To live with Him someday."

During the song I could hear a child's voice—someone close to me singing the words. The children up front were the only ones who were supposed to be singing. Supposing it was Wanda, I raised my head to tell her to be quiet.

But she wasn't singing. It was the voice of my dead brother. Clearly, I could hear his voice as he continued singing,

"I am a child of God,
Rich blessings are in store,
If I but learn to do his will,
I'll live with him once more..."

I put my face back into my hands and wept, knowing my brother's spirit lived and that I would see him again.

It's been 23 years since little Creed passed away. My life has certainly been different because of my faith and knowledge that life goes on after we die. After hearing Creed's voice, all desire to follow in the rebellious footsteps of my older brother left me.

Up until now I've never told anyone in the family about my experience at the funeral, but some recent events have lead me to write this down.

Recently I was watching a movie with my own five children. It was called *"Go Towards the Light,"* and was about a Mormon boy who was dying. As he was getting ready to die he said the exact same thing my brother, Creed, had said,

"Mommy, I'm dying. Pray for me. Mommy, I am dying."

I burst into tears and in my heart I cried, "Oh Creed, oh Creed."

My children looked at me, astonished, not used to seeing their father in tears. I went outside and went for a long walk in the mountains.

I've heard that the grieving process sometimes takes a long time, and to shed tears years after someone is gone is not unusual.

I want to share this story with my family—and with others too—for I think it will help those with heartaches over deceased loved ones. Even with the faith I have of living again, my grief over someone who has passed on is sometimes hard to bear. I hope this story might give comfort to others who have felt as I have felt over the loss of a loved one.

CHAPTER ELEVEN

Moroni Taught Him

by Fred Bohman

During the 1970's I was a purchasing agent for the LDS Church in South America, acquiring building maintenance and construction materials for the various church buildings. We lived in Quito, Ecuador.

I remember one day wandering through the marketplace. There were thousands of Indians crowding around hundreds of stalls where merchants peddled their wares. I was wearing jeans, a T-shirt and my French beret. I did not look like an American, let alone a typical employee of the LDS Church. It was my day off.

Suddenly I felt an unquestionable magnetism towards one of the stalls where a man was selling blankets and ponchos. As I walked closer, the man bent over; his coat fell open. I saw a little statue of Moroni hanging from a chain around his neck.

"You're a Mormon," I said.

"So are you," he replied.

"How can you tell?" I asked, surprised.

"I can tell," was his only response.

Segundo Moldanado and I became friends, not terribly close friends because he lived in Octavalo, a six hour journey from Quito. But there was an immediate liking and trust between us, though we spent little time together.

Several months later my wife Mary and I lost our first son. He was seven months old when he suffocated in his bed. We were sick with grief and guilt, wondering what we might have done to prevent the death.

It was at this very unhappy time that Segundo and his wife made the six-hour journey to Quito to see us. He said they had come to tell us of their conversion to the gospel and about the death of their son. They thought that by sharing their experiences with us we might find comfort and strength and a stronger faith in the afterlife.

Because they were Indians and used to speaking their native language, their Spanish was broken, but it was good enough for Mary and me to understand clearly what they were saying.

Their conversion to the church began in the late 60's when Elder Spencer W. Kimball sent missionaries to the Indian villages of Ecuador. Octavalo had about 20,000 inhabitants at the time, mostly Native Americans divided into family clans. The people still wore their native costumes and spoke their ancient languages. Octavalo was a clean city—the homes, the clothes people wore, everything. The people grew most of their own food, made most of their own clothing, and had little contact with the outside world.

When the first missionaries arrived in Octavalo they knocked on Segundo's door, showing him a Book of Mormon, telling him it was a history of his people.

"But I already know the history of my people," Segundo protested. "The record of my people was written on metal plates and buried in a mountain following a great battle."

The missionaries persisted until Segundo finally agreed to take the Book of Mormon. He was still very skeptical but agreed to read some of it.

When the missionaries were gone, Segundo picked up the book and began turning the pages, not reading, just thumbing through them. Suddenly pictures began forming in his mind, vivid color images of strange ships crossing stormy seas, great battles, prophets giving powerful sermons. He began hearing voices, then suddenly a personage was standing before him, a man in a white tunic which was open at the chest. The man was standing in the air about 18 inches off the ground.

The messenger taught Segundo out of the book. He also told him many things that were not in the book because they had been lost. Segundo said the messenger's name was Moroni.

When the missionaries returned, Segundo was ready to be baptized. Together they went down to the river where Segundo was baptized and confirmed. Soon afterwards the missionaries had to leave.

Segundo had a friend named Tabongo, who was accepting the gospel at the same time. Both were taught by Moroni. The persecutions began. Tabongo's wife and children left him. The local Catholic Church tried to disgrace him by sending priests to his home to cast out the devils they said he possessed. No one in Octavalo had ever joined the "Mormon Sect" before. Tabongo was barred from buying and selling in the marketplace. He was even tarred and feathered by a group of men from his neighborhood.

When the missionaries returned three weeks later, Tabongo was depressed and close to death. There was little they could say to bolster the spirits of the new convert. Soon they had to leave again.

The next time the missionaries returned, Tabongo was happier. His wife had returned and was ready to be baptized. She said that after she left her husband she had been taught by an angel, but it was not the same one that had taught her husband. The personage who had appeared to her and taught her the gospel was a gringo who, like her husband, had been taught by Moroni. The gringo's name was Joseph Smith.

Not very much later there was a major public confrontation between Tabongo and one of the Catholic priests. Tabongo called it a conflict of priesthoods. The priest tried to cast evil spirits out of Tabongo, who in return dusted off his feet in the direction of the priest, as a crowd of people watched. A short time after the confrontation the priest committed suicide. The gospel began to spread among the people with hundreds eventually joining the church.

Not long after Segundo had joined the church, he was in the marketplace one day, when his oldest son began screaming because of a terrible pain in his head. Within a few hours the son was dead.

Segundo and his wife were beside themselves with grief. One moment they wondered what they might have done to deserve this, the next they were angry with the Lord for allowing something so cruel and seemingly senseless to happen to their son.

They began fasting, determined to find out why it happened. They received no answer during an entire week of fasting. But they did not stop. They were determined to continue until they had an answer.

It was during the second week of the fast, while they were kneeling together in their hut, that it happened. The whole side of the house suddenly disappeared and they found themselves looking out into a beautiful garden full of flowers, trees, green grasses—the most beautiful place they had ever seen, but totally unfamiliar.

As they looked into the beautiful garden they saw their son who had died running towards them. He ran up to his parents, threw his arms around Segundo, saying,

"Don't worry about me. I had no choice but to go back."

Then they looked up and saw another man standing in a white robe, who said,

"Segundo, you have a righteous desire to know the fate of your son. The Lord has heard your prayers" This man, who showed them the wounds in his hands and feet, taught them for an hour or so until the vision or dream ended with the walls of the house closed in as they had been before.

After relating the story of his conversion, and the death of his son, Segundo looked at me and said,

"Fred, I know where your son is. He is with ours. He has specific tasks to perform. Don't worry."

Somehow my wife and I found comfort in those words. Thanks to Segundo we were able to believe more firmly that our son had not really died, but just passed on to a different kingdom where he needed to be.

Chapter Twelve

His Father Wouldn't Talk to Him

by Muriell Baldwin

My husband Marion had unusual spiritual qualities before he died. One time we were in the back yard of our Oroville, California area home when he suddenly asked me where the dog was. I said I didn't know. He asked me to help him find the dog and keep it in the yard, but whatever I did I was not to go out in the road. When I asked him what was wrong, he said a motorcycle was going to come too fast around the curve in front of our house and crash, and he didn't want me or the dog out there.

It wasn't very long after we had found the poodle and put it away that a young man on a motorcycle came around the corner out of control and crashed near our yard. As we ran over to help him, I felt grateful for my husband's foresight.

On the same day, Marion suddenly announced that our friends from Campbell, California, would be arriving within the hour. We hadn't talked to them in a long time, so I was naturally surprised at Marion's comment. When I asked him about it, he added that they would be coming in a new car.

"If you're so smart," I responded. "What color is the new car?"

"I don't know," he said, "except that it is a dark color. You know I'm color blind."

A short time later our friends pulled into the driveway in a brand new car. The color was a dark, royal blue.

During the 1970's Marion had increasing health problems, especially with his back and lungs. In 1971 he had to enter the Oroville Medical Center for a back operation.

It took a long time for him to return to his room from the operating room, and I was very worried about what might be going wrong. When the orderly finally rolled my husband in I asked why it had taken so long. He said there had been complications, but nothing more. I didn't think anything more of it.

A few days later as we were leaving the hospital, Marion told the doctor he wished he had taken a coffee break during the operation. Marion said that would have allowed him to stay longer at the beautiful place he had visited.

The doctor just laughed, but on the way home I asked Marion what he had been talking about. He told me that while they were operating on him he suddenly found himself going through a maze or misty tunnel at the end of which was a very bright light. After passing through the tunnel he came to the most beautiful park he had ever seen. The trees were in full bloom and the sun shining. He could smell the flowers, hear the birds and a trickling brook. This was a very peaceful place.

There was a park bench, and Marion's father, who had died in 1958, was sitting on it. Marion said as he was sitting down beside his father, he found his old black lunch box in his hand. He opened it and offered his father a sandwich. The father didn't accept the sandwich, nor did the old man acknowledge the presence of his son. Marion began to eat the sandwich himself.

All of a sudden my husband found himself shooting back through the tunnel and through the mist until he was in the operating room again, looking down on his body as they worked on him with the electric shock machine.

"Now I know why my chest hurt so badly," he thought as he watched them apply electricity to get his heart pumping again.

After the operation, when we went in for the first appointment with the doctor, he told us that Marion's heart had stopped for four minutes while he was on the operating table.

In mid October, 1978, he woke me up at 5 a.m. one morning to tell me about a dream he had had. He was told that if he would go back to Missouri he would live longer, though he wouldn't get well. He had a breathing problem that inhibited his oxygen intake to about 40 percent of normal.

"Do you want me to put the house up for sale?" I asked.

"No," he said. "I'm going to find out if the dream is from the Lord, and if it is, he will send someone to buy our house."

Two weeks later my neighbors, who were Mormons, had parents who came visiting from Utah. They drove up in a Honda, and started talking to my husband, and in the course of the conversation, asked Marion if he knew of any houses for sale. One thing led to another, and they bought our house. We headed for Missouri where we joined the LDS Church.

In 1981 we decided to come back to California to visit our friends. On our way home my Marion had a heart attack, that involved another out of body experience. He said he went through the mist and tunnel to the beautiful park, just like in the previous experience, and there sitting on the same bench was his father, holding our son, Marion Baldwin, Jr., who had died in 1967. Our son was born in 1963, and had never known Grandfather who had died in 1958.

Marion tried to talk to them, but they would not speak to him, nor would they acknowledge his presence.

In 1982 we received word from the Social Security Administration that they were coming around to check disabled people who were receiving disability. Marion became very upset because he was on 24-hour oxygen and didn't think they should be questioning the legitimacy of his disability. He had been a heavy duty crane operator.

"If they make me go back to work I don't know how I will do it," he said. I told him everything would be all right.

That night he had another out of body experience. He said he saw his body on the bed as he went into the mist and tunnel and back to the beautiful park. Again he saw his father, on the same bench, holding our son. Marion sat down by his father and told him how worried he was.

"Marion, don't worry about a thing. Everything will be taken care of," the father replied.

Marion was so happy that his father had finally talked to him. After returning to his body, Marion had no further worries about the upcoming visit from the Social Security Administration. This took place in the latter part of 1982.

Marion was diagnosed to have leukemia at that time, and he died in April of 1983 of that affliction, plus double pneumonia.

CHAPTER THIRTEEN

More Than a Dream

by J. Scott Winn,

I'm not exaggerating when I say my grandmother was my close friend. When I was five my mother had to go to work, and I refused to go to nursery school. Grandma intervened and invited me to stay with her and Grandpa. As busy as she was with farm chores and animals she always had time for me.

When I was ten we moved a quarter of a mile from them, and it seemed I was always with them evenings and weekends. One thing I remember about Grandma is her ability to work. She was always busy sewing, cooking, canning, cleaning and baking. She was always in motion.

One time I asked her why she always washed her knives and forks first when she did the dishes. She said that when she was a little girl she always hated to do them, so now she always washed them first so the job would be done and she could forget about it. That passed on to me. I too seem to want to do the unpleasant tasks first, so I can get them over with.

After my grandparents sold their farm, Grandma would come over to our house every day to do the dishes. We had a dishwasher, but she would always do them by hand. She cooked our evening meals. We all appreciated this because Mom and Dad were at work all the time.

As the years wore on, several strokes slowed Grandma down. I can still see her thin, 5'4" frame walking over to our house to do things for us. Eventually we found out she had stomach cancer and that there was nothing we could do for her. As her body filled with cancer she became confined to bed, but her spirit still soared. She knew what the outcome would be, but she wasn't afraid of death. She had told me that many times.

We knew the pain was unbearable, but she never uttered a word of complaint. Her only request was that someday we would have someone do her temple work for her.

One day as I knelt by her side she asked if she had been a good grandmother. All I could do was cry and say, "Yes, you are."

The next morning she passed quietly away in her sleep. I never felt as much hurt and loss as I felt that day. For weeks all I could do was think of the pain and suffering she had had to bear and how she had never complained about it.

Several weeks after her funeral, I awoke about 5 a.m. I lay wide awake for a long time until a deep sleep came over me. During this sleep my grandmother appeared to me, dressed in white, and said,

"Scott, don't worry, it doesn't hurt anymore. I've come to tell you I'm all right. It doesn't hurt anymore."

She held me tightly. In my mind I was yelling at myself to wake up. If I could just wake up, I knew Grandma was by my side. After she held me for a while she said she had to go.

After she departed I woke up. The feeling was overwhelming. I laid there with tears in my eyes. When my wife awakened and saw my emotional state, she asked if I had had a dream. I looked over at her and said I hadn't had a dream but a spiritual experience. Afterwards I wondered if maybe it was a dream after all, but when I think of her comment about my worrying, and the loving hug she gave me, I know deep in my heart that it was more than a dream. Where she had held me my flesh was still warm, just as if someone alive had been holding me. The feeling lasted throughout the day. I look forward to the day when we can meet again, and I can enjoy another one of those loving hugs.

Chapter Fourteen

The Golden Bridge

by Sherida Riggs

In July of 1974 I was scheduled to have plastic surgery on my face to correct a birth defect. I was a teenager at the time and had been through such surgeries before so I was pretty much familiar with the procedure the doctors were going to use on me.

At the time I had only been a member of the LDS Church for about two years and still had some doubts about my testimony of the gospel. The Sunday before the operation I was sitting in sacrament meeting next to my advisor, Sister Carol Wooten. I told her about the operation I was going to have and she asked me if I had had a blessing. I said no, that I didn't really know much about that or how to go about getting a blessing.

After the meeting she took me into the bishop's office. They had just finished a meeting and some of the elders were still there, so the bishop invited them to help with the blessing.

I will never forget the feeling I had when those men placed their hands on my head. A warm, peaceful feeling started from the top of my head and went all the way down to my toes. I felt the spirit of the Lord with me. I don't remember what was said in the blessing but I will always feel the warmth of the spirit that was present in the room.

The next day in the hospital everything started out well. I remember being wheeled into the operating room and being conscious during the operation. After the surgery was over I was wheeled back to my room. I seem to remember that I then dozed off to sleep.

Shortly after that, as I learned later, my friend Rose Ann arrived at the hospital to be with me as I recovered. She said that when she approached the bed I appeared unconscious with my eyes half closed and my lips blue. She was afraid to try to wake me, so she just sat there in the chair and waited for me to wake up by myself.

Just then a nurse walked into the room to wake me for dinner. When she saw my condition she called a code 99, indicating an emergency.

Rose Ann was rushed out of the room and the girl in the next bed was moved, bed and all, out in the hallway to make room for the resuscitating equipment. Rose Ann said that the doctors worked on me for quite a while, until I screamed. They told me to scream again. Not long after that I awakened, seeing two strange doctors at the foot of my bed, and my parents beside the bed.

At the time, I couldn't remember anything that had happened. I only knew what Rose Ann and my parents told me. But with the passing of time, strange flashbacks in my memory, or dreams, would come to me.

I saw a bridge. It wasn't like any bridge I had ever seen in my life. It was the most beautiful piece of architecture anyone could imagine. It was fashioned somewhat like the Golden Gate Bridge in San Francisco, except that the one in my memory was actually made of gold, or at least part of it. The span was of pure marble and the cables were pure gold. It was suspended in mid air with clouds or fog around it.

I remember standing above it in the air looking down on it. There was someone standing beside me showing me the bridge.

There were people walking back and forth across the bridge. It was wide enough to allow the people to walk three abreast in both directions. There were a lot of people on the bridge, and they were all dressed in white. I don't remember anything about leaving my body or returning to it. Perhaps with the passing of time I will remember more.

I kept seeing this bridge in my memory and dreams, like some kind of recurring flashback. I didn't understand what it could mean. Then one day I was reading in the scriptures about a bridge that linked the different levels of the spirit world together. Suddenly it hit me like a lightning bolt that I had seen this connecting bridge, and the memory of it was fresh in my mind and memory.

Somewhere along the way I lost the scriptural reference to the bridge, and have been unable to find it again. But the feeling of peace each time I "see" the bridge in my mind is still there. I am no longer afraid to die. I know there is life beyond this earthly existence.

CHAPTER FIFTEEN

I Recognized Their Faces

Ronna Lackey

I have had thirteen surgeries so far in my life. Good health is not one of my privileges; going beyond the veil, for some strange reason, seems to be. Not that I really want it that way. I wish there was some kind of happy medium.

Nearly sixteen years ago I had surgery to disconnect or cut some of the nerves at the base of my skull because of pain I was experiencing. The pain had slowly built over the years from two car accidents I had been in. By severing the nerves I would only have feeling in my face.

I was supposed to lay flat for forty-eight hours after the surgey, but without really thinking I raised the hospital bed. I guess it was more of an unconscious act. Suddenly I was stabbed with severe pain. I laid the bed back and became very dizzy. Things went black and then I felt a very peaceful feeling. There was a weightlessness I couldn't understand.

A brightness appeared over my head. I heard a voice and looked up. The light above was almost too bright to look at. It also looked somewhat misty.

As I looked through the mist I saw a man. He reached down with his right hand and took my left hand. I felt extreme peace and love. He told me everything was all right and that I should come with him. I floated out of my body up to him. As I floated beside him I turned, looked down and saw my body. It was very startling. I couldn't understand what was happening. He understood what I was thinking and began to comfort me. He told me not to worry, everything was all right.

I began to question my feelings. I felt extremely peaceful. I had not experienced that much love before. It seemed to be coming from everywhere. I was also aware of pure knowledge. Things went quickly through my mind. I could understand many things.

He told me that the knowledge I had gained about life and death since being a member of the church was true. When he spoke, I not only received the thoughts in my mind but I also saw what he was saying, like pictures. Whenever he talked about parts of my life I could see those events.

We reviewed my whole life. He showed me the struggles that I had gone through. As we went through each experience, I felt his hurt when I had hurt. He comprehended totally everything I had suffered and experienced. He talked about an illness I had while in my early twenties. I was not a member of the church then. I was told by the doctors that I would probably not make it. I had a liver disease and I asked God to allow me to be with my children and raise them. That request had been granted and I was healed.

He also told me about time. It seemed that I was with him for nearly an hour, but it couldn't have been more than about two-and-a-half minutes.

When it was completed, I said I didn't want to go back to my present struggles and illness. I didn't want to go back to my body. He asked if I had raised my children. He asked in a teaching way not because he needed to know. I was aware he already knew. I said,

"No."

"Then you will have to go back," He explained.

I tried to convince him to let me stay. I was pleading not to return to all that pain but was told I had more to do. As I looked at him, his love was so overwhelming I almost couldn't stand it. It was ten times overwhelming. It was like a wave rushing over me. I felt I would burst with his love and I knew I couldn't refuse.

I looked down again at my body and saw a nurse come in my room. She saw my condition and ran out. I saw another nurse and a doctor run in. I then felt myself going down to my body.

I felt so encapsulated, restricted or entombed. Everything was very heavy. I felt the pain. I opened my eyes and saw the doctors and nurses. They couldn't believe I had come back. They were getting ready to use the electrodes.

I will never forget the exquisite peace and love that nearly consumed me but persuaded me to continue on.

In 1985, I was again in the hospital, this time for malignant adhesions on my large and small bowels. During the three months in the hospital I had my eighth, ninth and tenth operations. The adhesions had grown around some of my organs. They did the best they could to cut around things. Some of the growths were extremely difficult to cut. My small bowels were almost completely destroyed.

I was severely malnourished. The pain from the bowel obstructions was excruciating. It was worse than child birth, kidney or gall stones, because I've experienced all of those, too. In the middle of this debilitating pain, I suddenly rose up out of my body. There was no one there to greet me. I didn't need an escort this time, because I had already been there. The brightness was a little different. I felt the same peacefulness and relief from pain. I also felt the same quickness of mind and freedom.

The brightness was somewhat foggy as I proceeded. I was compelled to push myself forward. In that state you don't walk, you are propelled by your mind. In a way, you walk with your thought processes.

The more I went forward through the mist the more I was enveloped by peace and contentment. I couldn't see through the haze but became aware of the outline of a person which was more vivid as I got closer. I saw another person and another until I saw an extremely large group.

I didn't recognize anyone. I was wondering who they were. A woman stood in front of the group and read my thoughts and communicated to me with her thoughts. She was aware of the other experiences in my life and helped me remember them. She helped me see and remember experiences that I can't recall now.

Sometimes I have read the scriptures and understood a concept and then realized she explained it to me. I understood it because I had been shown, but I didn't recall it until I came across it in the scriptures.

While I was with the group I felt so much love from them, I wondered why. They weren't people I knew. Who was I to them? The woman in front ascertained my thoughts and questions and said the group had been praying for me.

That was a new thought. I didn't know spirits prayed. She told me that I would understand my questions later. She communicated more and as she did, I saw the image.

I felt a great yearning of emotion from the woman and the group. I understood that I had chosen to live now and had promised to do certain work. I thought,

"I don't even know what it is".

The woman told me it would become clear to me as time went on.

"But remember you promised", she repeated, time and time again. I felt the weight of this promise and knew I couldn't stay without filling it. I had to go back to earth to keep that promise.

She opened up a vision and showed me a basket of flowers. If I returned to the spirit world without fulfilling my promise I would be returning with an empty basket—without any flowers. I saw myself approaching Father in Heaven with my small empty basket and my head hung in shame. I could not bear it.

Since returning I have worked hard so that I will not have to hang my head. I want my basket full when I return to Him.

The vision closed and she explained that it was time for me to go back. I said,

"But who are you?"

She told me I would understand later.

I felt myself going backward very quickly. I perceived the yearning of the group and their love as I left. I was reminded they would be praying for me. Immediately I was back in my body and the pain was unbelievable.

Two years later my aunt died. She left a large cedar chest or hope chest to my sister, who was not then a member of the church. The cedar chest was full of pictures of relatives, acquaintances and friends of the family. I wanted to get the pictures and do the genealogy for those people. I had done a little genealogy before. My mother, also not a member, helped me get the chest.

I was in extremely poor health. I was on Demerol and an I.V. I prayed and prayed that the spirit would be with me and help me. It required an extreme amount of effort. As I went through the pictures it was amazing. Though I had never met most of the people, I knew who they were. I recognized them as members of the group I had seen beyond the veil. I knew their names and where they fit in each family tree. As I worked on each individual I felt that person communicating with me in my mind. I eventually filled fifteen large binders of genealogy from those pictures and the information in the chest.

A year-and-a-half ago I sold my baby-grand piano and whatever else was of value and went to New Mexico to validate the work that I had done. I met relatives I didn't know and some I thought were dead.

As the families went through the albums they asked, "How did you get these names right?" They were amazed that I had everyone in the right place. I can only attribute it to my special privilege of a trip beyond the veil and seeing at least some of my purpose in this life.

CHAPTER SIXTEEN

She Always Had A Smile For Me

by Robin Bloodworth

When I turned 18, I had to start attending relief society meetings. I was hesitant to go. None of the sisters was my age. They were all older. The presidency tried to make me feel comfortable, make me feel as if I belonged.

One woman in particular, Christine, went out of her way to make me feel welcome. She was one of the counselors. When I'd walk in the door every Sunday, she always had a smile for me and everyone else. I never remember seeing her upset about anything.

Christine had a beautiful husband and four healthy boys. All of them were active in the church. They seemed like a very happy family.

All of a sudden Christine stopped coming to church.I couldn't understand why. Eventually I found out she had a sickness that was keeping her away. She didn't have the strength to come. At first I didn't think it was very serious, that she would pull through and soon be back with us.

After a while I heard she had been transferred to the hospital in Tucson, Arizona. She had lupus, and there were specialists and equipment for treating her condition in Tucson.

I never did go down there to see her because I believed she would soon get better and be coming back to church. But every time I heard a report on her condition she seemed to be getting worse. I heard from others that her goal that year was to be home for Christmas. The holiday season came and went with Christine still in the hospital.

One day as I arrived home from work there was a get-well card on the table. My mother had purchased it to give to Christine. Mom had never known Christine very well, so I asked her why she had purchased it. She said she didn't know, just that she felt like doing it. We signed it and sent it off.

The card arrived at the hospital on January 4, 1989. Christine died that night.

Though I had hardly known the woman, I felt like I had lost my best friend. The only interaction between us had been some friendly interchanges at church. Yet I will never forget how I felt when I heard she had died. The grief was overwhelming. I also worried about her husband and boys and how difficult a time they must be having, realizing they had probably known for some time she was going to die.

Going to her funeral was a very difficult thing for me. I had always tried to avoid funerals, but I felt I had to go to Christine's. After the funeral I couldn't get her out of my mind.

About a week later, I was in bed one night, wondering if Christine was happy. As I went to sleep I found myself in a dream condition, walking towards a garage door. I could see Christine's husband and four boys in their car. Their faces were dazed. As I continued to walk towards them, I got the strongest feeling that I needed to look back over my shoulder. As I did everything went black. When I looked back at the car, there was a bright light over the front passenger seat. The husband and boys were gone. Christine was sitting directly under the light.

I often dream about people I don't know, so I remember asking myself if this was really Christine. I took a very close look. It was her. I looked into her eyes, and she into mine. All of a sudden the car backed out of the garage. Christine had the biggest smile on her face, just like I remembered it.

When I awakened I knew she was happy. She knows that she will be with her family again. She watches them everyday. And she watches over her friends, too. Even though I didn't know her that well, I can't wait to see Christine again, when I proceed beyond the veil.

Chapter Seventeen

Daddy Was There With Us Today

by Doris Quiroz

Our son, Ricky, was born March 9, 1977. He was very ill and shortly after his birth was put in an incubator and taken by ambulance to Cedar Sinai Hospital's neonatal unit in Los Angeles, California.

Before they took him, they allowed my husband and me to look and touch him through the openings in the incubator. They said they didn't expect him to survive the trip. My husband had tears in his eyes and was trying to be brave for me because I was lying flat on the guerney following a caesarean birth. I looked up at him with the strongest conviction I could muster, and said, "God is not going to take our son from us."

Ricky was our third child. We had two lovely little girls at home: Laura, five, and Linda, soon to be three. My husband adored his daughters but was excited to finally get a son.

During the following three days, Ricky was in critical condition and the prognosis hadn't changed. At that time we were not members of the LDS Church, but I had read some months earlier about laying on hands for healing. I had a strong desire to be with my son to try to do more than was medically possible. The doctor was reluctant to let me go so soon, but since I was determined to go, he had no choice but to release me.

After leaving the hospital we drove in silence to Cedars and my husband borrowed a wheelchair to take me up to where Ricky was. He was lying on a warming table with tubes everywhere. He looked so helpless.

He seemed to respond immediately to my voice, and when I first placed my hands on his little chest I was startled to feel his ribs so pronounced as his little chest heaved up and down from the force of the respirator.

I bowed my head and prayed fervently to my Father in Heaven to provide me with the power to heal my son through my hands. When I was finished my husband asked what I had been doing, and I answered, "The only thing I know how to do—pray."

The ride home took about thirty minutes. Just as we entered the home, the phone rang. It was a nurse from the hospital saying our son had taken a turn for the good. She said he had started breathing on his own, with the respirator accounting for only about 50 percent of his breathing. Earlier it had been at 98 percent. She said he was still in critical condition, but that he now had a chance of surviving.

And survive he did, with no side effects. On the day of his homecoming, we stopped by a church to give thanks on the way home. When we looked at Ricky, we were amazed how much he looked like his father.

Two months after Ricky's third birthday, his father was killed in an automobile accident.

As we mourned, friends came by to console us. While my daughters allowed themselves to be consoled, Ricky—normally a very active child—stood stoically at my side. He didn't understand the concept of death. I tried to explain that God had taken his father and that someday we'd be together again.

After the mourning period was over, Ricky's longing for his Daddy turned to anger. He felt his father had abandoned us, and hurt us. He hated his father and also God for having taken him.

I was distraught, not sure how to handle Ricky's bitterness. We sought counseling. I was told he was too young to comprehend, that his feelings were natural. In time he would realize his father hadn't had a choice in the matter.

In a way this came to pass, but not like I thought it would. Ricky's anger was replaced with indifference. Other kids had dads, but he didn't, and he didn't care either. He retreated into his own world.

I tried to be supermom. I made sure he went out for every sport. He was in scouts—and everything other boys did, he did too. I always told him how much he looked like his father. Ricky's mannerisms were similar too—serious, conscientious, neat and orderly, even in the way he kept his bedroom. His things were just so. He was cautious and caring. When I would attempt to complement Ricky on these characteristics, he would just shrug his shoulders and say, "So?"

Then one Sunday it all changed. We were in fast and testimony meeting the week before general conference. As we were sitting there after the sacrament, the first person to bear testimony was Carol Christensen, the wife of our stake president. She talked about what a special blessing it had been to have a general authority stay in their home recently.

Next, was her son, Lance, whom I thought was also going to speak about the general authority. But instead, he gave a beautiful and tender testimony of his father. He spoke of the love and support he received from his father, and about the father's blessing he had received at the beginning of the school year. I enjoyed his testimony, and the others, that day, but didn't notice anything out of the ordinary.

After we had been home several hours, in a very serious voice, Ricky said,

"Didn't you feel Daddy there with us today?"

"Where?" I asked.

"There, in church," he replied. "In sacrament meeting, and he was with me during my other classes too." He added that the experience made him feel sad, like crying.

"Where did he sit?" I asked, startled at what Ricky was telling me. "Did he sit next to you, between us, on the aisle?"

"No, not like that," Ricky said. "He was just there."

"Did you see his face?" I asked. "Was he wearing white clothes?"

"No, no," he replied. "I just saw his face. That's all."

"Was his hair long or short?"

"No, I didn't see his hair, only his face."

"Did he have a mustache?" I asked.

"No, he didn't."

My husband had always worn a mustache, plainly visible in all the pictures we had of him, but he had shaved it off just before he was killed.

I knew Ricky had felt his father's spirit and seen his face. Innocence had seen through the veil.

"Did he whisper to you?" I asked.

Ricky answered very seriously that his father hadn't whispered to him, just that a good feeling had come over him. At that moment I remembered Lance's testimony about his father, and said to Ricky that his father wanted him to know that he loved and blessed his son just like Lance's father did.

I was overwhelmed with the idea that love indeed can reach across the barrier separating life and death.

Chapter Eighteen

He Called Me Bobby Ann

by Barbara Ross

It was a December Wednesday, an average workday morning, 1976. I was on my way to work. I remember thinking of all the things I had to do that day, hoping everything would fit together so I could get them all done.

I was an educational consultant with several meetings and inservice appointments planned with teachers that day. I was reviewing all this in my mind when a car pulled out in front of me. I was on a four-lane highway traveling in the left-hand lane.

It was a cloudy morning with patches of fog settling on the road, resulting in slippery spots. Seeing the car pull in front of me, I hit the brakes. My car began spinning, turning around in the road, crossing the opposing lanes of traffic, sliding into a field and striking an old cement foundation which caused the car to roll into a tree.

For a moment, after hitting the foundation, it seemed I was above the car, watching it roll across the field into the tree. Then everything was quiet. Maybe I was unconscious, at least catching my breath.

When I regained my senses, I knew I was trapped in the car prone on my back. It didn't appear there was much damage from my position under the dash. I remember thinking it strange that the windshield wasn't even broken. Later I learned the car was totally demolished and the windshield broken into a thousand pieces. When I tried to move, I couldn't.

I decided I had to let people know I was there, knowing I was quite a distance from the road. I started honking the horn as best I could. I picked a rhythm, so those hearing it would know the honking was deliberate, not just a stuck horn.

Eventually a young man came to the car, looked down and shook his head. I gave him the phone numbers of my work place and my husband's work place, and asked him to please call. He just shook his head and left. I wasn't sure if he was going to make the calls so I started blowing the horn again.

A few minutes later I looked up and saw people I knew, plus a state policeman. They were looking down at me rather strangely. I didn't know why they were looking that way. I suppose it might have been the incoherent way I was talking. I asked the officer to please be sure there was no mention of the accident in the newspaper.

Soon an ambulance came. A young man and woman pulled me out of the car. They said they thought my legs were hurt. I found out later my thigh bone was broken, as was my pelvis in three places. The ball joint had been pushed right through the socket. Three ribs on my left side were broken too. There were particles of glass in my face, a collapsed lung, ruptured spleen, and internal bleeding so profuse that later in the hospital I consumed 30 pints of blood during two operations.

I remember the ambulance ride to the hospital, and being taken into emergency, where I waited from 9 a.m. until 5 p.m. for a surgeon to become available to operate. In the meantime they began cleaning up my face, mostly small chunks of glass in my mouth and stuck in the skin. They began giving me fluids through a needle in my arm.

I remember looking up at a doctor who had sweat on his face as he called for another doctor. He was calling for a surgeon. He knew I was bleeding internally and had broken bones.

I remember wishing it would hurt more so I could pass out and not have to experience everything that was going on. For a while I seemed to be going in and out of consciousness. I couldn't talk or express myself, but I seemed to hear everything that was going on. I remember the following conversation between two of the people working on me.

"She came in in pretty bad shape, and if we don't get busy she'll go out in a canvas bag," said one voice.

"Let's get busy," said another voice.

I was reminded of when I was a little girl watching my uncles catch and clean fish. I could hear the same kinds of sounds, as when my uncles cut open and cleaned their fish. I didn't know what the doctors were doing to me.

It was quiet, or blank, for a while, then I heard a voice say, "What's her blood pressure?"

"Thirty over zero," was the reply.

"Come on you fools," I remember thinking, "Those numbers are not blood pressure readings. They may have something to do with the weather outside, but not my blood pressure."

"We better get moving on this," a voice said. "If we don't, we'll lose her."

The next thing I remember is sliding down a trough or slide. At a certain point I remember being very reluctant, feeling cold. There was a strange sound, not quite like a siren or whistle, but very loud and unlike any sound I had ever heard before.

When I got to the bottom of the slide I was suddenly warm. My surroundings were beautiful, like a garden—with flowers, lawn, trees, etc. It reminded me of a park by the river where I had gone as a child for family reunions. There were people visiting and walking about.

I saw my father sitting on one of the benches. I went over to him. I remember communicating with him. I don't say talking, because I don't remember hearing any sounds.

"Daddy, please let me stay," I asked. "Please let me stay. I don't want to go back. It will hurt too much. I don't want to go through all that. I just want to stay here."

I could feel the peace and beauty of the place. The people were calm and happy. It was kind of like a college campus. I could feel a warm, accepting atmosphere.

My father was shaking his head and looking at me, not saying anything. Then my grandmother appeared, telling me I couldn't stay. She said I had to go back, that I wasn't finished yet. I told her I didn't want to go back, that I wanted to stay. Yet, somehow I knew she had the final word. She had always been a forceful, authoritative person, who believed you did the things that were hard to do because they were right. I knew I had to go back.

My father looked just like he had looked the last time I saw him, pretty much in the prime of his life, calm and in control. Grandmother looked harassed and harried, kind of tense. I remember her being that way before she died. I got the feeling that she wasn't at as high a level of spiritual development as my father was. She had come from a different part of the afterworld, from a group of people who were unsettled like she was, less distinct in their appearance, and not as much in control as my father. He was benign and calm, like he had been in life.

Though I don't remember this part, one of my friends who visited me immediately following the surgery said I told her I had visited with my father who had called me by the nick name that only he called me, Bobby Ann. She said I told her that my father said I had to go back because I had other work to do. When I asked him what the work was, his only response was that I would know. That was all he could say at that time.

After the discussions with my father and grandmother, the next thing I remember was waking up in my hospital bed and looking into the faces of relatives.

The orthopedic physician who operated on me came in one day and said,

"I can't forget who you are. You are the one who went to the other side. Everything shut down. You had no vital signs. Do you know who was in the Jesus seat?"

"No."

"The anesthesiologist. He brought you back."

I wanted to disagree with him, tell him that it was my father and grandmother who made me come back, but instead I said nothing, figuring he probably wouldn't understand the things that go on beyond the veil.

Chapter Nineteen

The Strangers Embraced Me

by Doreen Edwards

When I was about seven years old I had a playmate named Dennis. He lived next door to us in Edgbaston, Warwick, England. Dennis's mother died that year. It was customary in England at that time for close friends and relatives to pay last respects at the home before the body was taken to the funeral parlor.

I remember my mother going next door to see Dennis' mother for the last time. I was not allowed to go because I was too young.

When mother returned she was sad and upset. I tried to comfort her by saying,

"I'm sure she was happy that you came. I wish I could have gone with you."

My comment only made my mother angry.

"She couldn't have been happy, or sad, or anything else," Mother replied. "She is dead. Her life is over, finished."

"When someone dies they can still hear and see, just not respond," I argued. I don't know where the idea came from, only that I had not been taught that at home.

"Absolutely not," Mother insisted. "When you die your life comes to an end. You are no more."

I was a child and she was an adult so, of course, she won the argument. As a result I became very much afraid of death, especially two years later, at age nine, when I became seriously ill with pluerisy and double pneumonia. I had had many illnesses as a child. I received all the medication available, but still did not get well.

The doctor visited our home one evening and after examining me, told my mother, as I found out later, that I would probably not live through the night, that my death could come at any moment. He told her to make me as comfortable as possible, and recommended extra hot water bottles on my chest and along my sides.

About an hour after the doctor's departure the pain became even more intense, so my mother decided to go next door to fetch another hot water bottle.

Though I hadn't heard what the doctor had said, I was crying that I didn't want to die. I was afraid to die. I was terrified. My mother tried to comfort me, telling me I was not going to die. I remember continuing to cry as she went next door to borrow the hot water bottle.

Shortly after Mother left the room the pain became unbearable. Even crying brought agony. I remember for a few seconds trying to catch my breath, then suddenly the pain was gone, completely.

At first I thought I might have fallen asleep. Then I realized I was looking down on myself in my bed. I could see the bedroom door behind my bed, the entire house, in front of the house, and my mother in the house next door talking to the neighbor. I felt so peaceful and good.

Then I was aware that I was not alone. People were gathering around me, and welcoming me. I felt surrounded by so much love. They were dressed in white and some of them embraced me. I felt so happy. I didn't know who the people were, but I felt like I knew them and they knew me. Together we began moving towards a white light.

"No, no, she has to go back," said a voice, stopping our progress towards the light.

"No, I don't want to go back," I protested.

"You must return." The voice was strong, but not loud, the kind of voice you don't argue with. Three times it told me I must return.

I could see my body again, in the bedroom. I saw my mother return from the neighbors, climb the stairs, and go over to me on the bed. She took my hand, presumably to check my pulse. Then she dropped my arm back on the bed. She turned briefly toward the window.

My bedroom window had been open, and when she had noticed from the neighbors that I had stopped crying, she had hurried home. Unable to feel my pulse, she turned towards the window to gather her strength.

Suddenly all the pain was back again, and I was hurting and crying. Mother hurried back to my bed.

As I became well I did not tell anyone about my experience. In fact I kept it to myself for many years, fearing ridicule, not wanting people to think I was crazy. Yet I could not forget that experience and the wonderful feelings of love and peace I experienced for just a short while.

It wasn't until I joined the LDS Church, at age twenty-one in Australia, that I found religious doctrine that was consistent with my experience. I knew my spirit had left my body for a short while, then returned again. The terror I had of death is gone.

Chapter Twenty

I Was Allowed to Say Goodby

by Janice Vande Merwe

In August of 1978 my eighteen-year-old daughter, Janill, and her friend, Diane Lander, were vacationing with two other girl friends in Wildwood, New Jersey. They were trying to spend as much time together as possible before returning to college. Janill was returning to Ricks College in Idaho and would not be seeing her friends again until Christmas. Even though the girls were busy in family activities, and preparing for college, they were determined to squeeze in one more trip to the beach before summer ended.

Torn between wanting to spend as much time in the sun as possible, and having to return to our home in Chambersburg, Pennsylvania for a wedding the next day, they decided to stay at the beach until the sun went down, then drive through the night so as to be home for the wedding.

It was on their way home from the beach on Saturday morning that Diane, in the early morning hours, on the Pennsylvania Turnpike, became disoriented, or perhaps fell asleep at the wheel. Their car drifted into oncoming traffic and collided head-on with a fifty-foot motor home.

They both were killed instantly, and I can't begin to measure the great loss it was for us, the death of our only daughter.

We were in shock as we went through the formalities of the viewings, funeral services and burials for both girls. The adjustment to having one of our children severed so quickly from our presence was proving to be too much for me. Everything I had ever learned about the plan of salvation and the hereafter was not enough to give me comfort in the absence of my daughter.

I went through all the phases of grieving, even blaming myself for letting her go on the needless vacation. We had been out of town when they left, and I hadn't even been able to say goodby to her.

I was praying for the comforter to do what the scriptures had promised—to give comfort. But comfort did not come, and I was beginning to have problems with my health. It became clear to me how someone could literally die from a broken heart.

I knew now what it was to have a broken heart and a contrite spirit. I was suffering deeply, and in the process was repenting from everything I had ever done contrary to gospel principles. I read the scriptures every day, and prayed all the time. I read all the books I could find about life after life. I felt that at least my thoughts would be with her, if I knew all about her new life.

One night as I was sleeping, I became aware that I was floating about a foot above the bed. I was still lying in a prone position, but above the covers.

I was aware of many colors in the room—beautiful pastel colors like I had never seen before. Janill was standing in the doorway, smiling at me. She was different in that she too was very colorful, bathed in pastel shades of light. She was aglow with light, and her happiness was obvious.

I don't remember going to her. All I know is that all of a sudden I was with her. We hugged each other. We were both standing above the floor. Nothing was said, but somehow I knew she had come to let me know she was happy, and that everything would be all right.

I felt extremely happy and peaceful. A feeling of total acceptance and forgiveness came over me. I knew without a shadow of a doubt that the accident was no one's fault. It had just happened. I told her that I loved her and missed her. Then we both said goodby.

When I awoke I was in bed again. I remember thinking how heavy my body felt. I awakened my husband and told him what had happened. We prayed together, and I fell asleep again. The next thing I knew I was floating above the bed again, and the exact same thing happened again.

I am grateful to my Father in Heaven for allowing that short visit from beyond the veil. I will always remember the feelings of love and peace I felt that night. I know that my mortal eyes could never have seen her, but only my spiritual eyes—and that my life was changed forever.

I have had dreams of Janill many times since that night, but none have been so real, nor felt as peaceful. None have had the colors, nor has she ever been so aglow with light and happiness as the night my spirit was allowed to visit my daughter beyond the veil.

Chapter Twenty-One

Death is a Part of Life

by Thelma T. Huffman

Death is really a beautiful thing, an experience to look forward to and never to fear. I know because I died nearly 40 years ago. In fact, the *Salt Lake Tribune* reported me as Weber County's sixteenth auto death in 1949.

I didn't suspect death was racing toward me that day on Highway 89 south of Ogden. As I was nearing a turn in the highway, I was met by a speeding gasoline truck pulling a semi-trailer. He hit his brakes, and with the road surface slick from rain, his trailer jack-knifed and slammed into my car.

A Utah state trooper found me pinned inside my smashed car, broken and bleeding, my head hanging out the window. When he finally managed to remove me from the twisted wreckage, he carried me to the side of the road and covered my body, including my face, with a blanket.

He then listed me on his report as dead at the scene of the accident, and the next day, October 10, 1949, the *Salt Lake Tribune* reported that I had been killed.

Lying bloody there by the road, I felt my life ebbing away, my strength fading. I could feel myself slipping from this life. I was dying—and it was wonderful. No earthly feeling can compare with the heavenly peace that filled me.

Suddenly, I realized I was high above the scene of the accident, watching what was going on below me.

Cheryl, my four-year-old daughter had been in the back seat. She was suffering from severe shock, cuts and abrasions. From my vantage point above the scene of the accident, I saw a lady in a black car stop. The lady put Cheryl into her car. I somehow knew she was a kind lady and would take good care of my daughter. She took her to the hospital where they cleaned her up and kept her overnight for observation.

I was overwhelmed with a feeling of utter blissfulness. Beautiful people—many of them old friends—gathered around me. We were together, above the scene of the accident, looking down. We were all in a shaft of light, and it extended to the ground, covering the area of the accident.

We didn't need words to communicate. They knew and I knew what was happening.

My life flashed before me. I was experiencing judgment. Among other things I learned that the most important thing we can do on this earth is to show consideration, love and kindness to others. There are no bonuses for position alone, nor power and wealth. We are judged by how we treat people, and what we do for others. I learned that heavenly judgment is a learning experience and nothing to fear. It was wonderful.

I understood that I had a choice to make. I could remain with these beautiful people or return to the broken, pain-racked body at the side of the road.

My mind rebelled at the thought of going back. I didn't want to leave the bliss that surrounded me. Furthermore, I didn't have the courage to go back; but as I thought about my husband and three little children, I knew what I had to do.

I prayed and asked for the courage to want to live. Instantly, it was given to me. Suddenly I could feel the courage and desire to live in every fiber of my being. And then something wonderful happened—I was promised that I would live and raise my children. This was a promise with no conditions attached.

I remember thinking that if someone suddenly came along with an axe and decided to cut the head off my body, they would not be able to do it because God had promised me that I would live and raise my children. I felt the spirit of the Lord with me as plainly as I feel the keys on this typewriter. I was no longer afraid of anything.

I was impressed, however, to know that it would take a long time to recover. I knew the easiest thing to do would be stay where I was and not go back. I knew too that there were important lessons for me to learn during the healing process. I later learned that soul cleansing can come through illness.

I watched from above as they loaded my body into the ambulance. As the ambulance was on the way up the hill, I finished my prayer for courage and my spirit reentered my tortured body. But I didn't go alone to the hospital—one of the beautiful people I had met on the other side came with me to encourage and support me. She wore an exquisite, white robe with a sash of the same whiteness.

At the hospital, doctors found my injuries included a fractured skull with a punctured eardrum, a concussion, a double compound comminuted fracture of the left thigh, crushed left knee cap, severed tendon, broken right forearm, compound fractured jaw, a broken nose, and loosened front teeth.

They had little hope of my living. But with a strange certainty, I knew I would survive. During that first week, I was told by a beautiful voice that I would live, be well, and raise my children.

It could be thought, considering the condition of my body, that that first week would have been especially hellish, but it wasn't. It was really beautiful and serene. I was somehow able to detatch myself from the pain and enjoy the serenity and peace that I had felt during the brief period I was outside my body. It was after the first week that the trials seemed to set in.

As I had been warned, the healing process was slow. In order to repair my jaws, they had to wire them shut. I lost a lot of weight because it was so difficult to get nourishment. Once a nurse gave me a shot and the needle came out bent at an extreme angle because of lack of flesh. My only food was liquids, and I had a difficult time drinking the sweet juices they gave me. Sometimes I would ask for a blessing on my glass of juice so I could drink it. I realized that I needed heavenly help if I was not going to starve.

I remember well when the doctor finally, after several months, took the wires off my jaws, and I could open my mouth wide enough to put solid food into it. Previously, all nourishment had to be obtained by sucking the liquids through my teeth. The wire holding my jaw and teeth in place would not even allow a straw inside.

The day they removed the wires, they gave me a soft-boiled egg for breakfast. I had never liked soft boiled eggs before, but that morning that egg tasted better than anything I had ever tasted in my entire life. The nurses on the floor came in to watch me eat that first breakfast, and rejoice with me over the fact that I could now open my mouth and eat, at least soft foods.

One day blood clots went from my leg to my lungs, cutting off my breathing so that I was gasping for air. Sharp pains accompanied each gasp. My bishop and one of his counselors came in, placed their hands on my head, and gave me a blessing. During the administration I started breathing with deep breaths, comfortably and without pain. Later, the doctors removed the oxygen tent. They said the blood clots were gone. I realized once more how totally dependent I was upon the Lord for my recovery.

Another day I became very angry at one of the nurses for giving me a pain shot without my knowledge. Later in the day I realized that if I allowed myself to become angry I certainly could retard my recovery. The Lord had permitted me to come back to raise my children, but it was up to me to keep anger, resentment and lack of forgiveness out of my heart.

I prayed about it and received an instant answer. Prolonged anger and feelings of hate can canker the soul, I realized. Then I felt cleansed, completely released from the anger. This took no mental effort on my part. It was gone and in its place was understanding and love for the nurse. I told myself she had only had my welfare in mind in doing what she did. When she came back to the hospital room, I apologized to her and told her that I loved her. We had a good talk and became the best of friends. She told me she had just moved into the area and had been so lonely until she met me.

After many weeks in the hospital, I became terribly homesick. I wanted to go home so badly I began begging the doctors to let me go. The nurses thought it was a foolish thing for me to do because I was so helpless. In fact, I couldn't even turn over in bed because of the way my leg was set with pins.

The doctor lived across the street from us so he figured he could look in on me frequently. His wife was a nurse and she could come over every day.

Finally, a week before Christmas, after sixty-eight days in the hospital, I went home. No one could have been happier than I was. I thought returning home was the nicest thing that had ever happened to me. My husband had arranged for a hospital bed and I just lay there and looked around and thanked my Heavenly Father that I was finally home.

After being home only a few days, I developed a high fever and a sickness almost like the flu, with chills and fever included. Infection was oozing from around one of the pins. The smell was terrible.

Virginia, the nurse from across the street, gave me penicillin shots every day for eleven days but with no relief. The doctor made arrangements for me to go back to the hospital the next day.

I could not bring myself to go back—I couldn't stand the thought of it. It was too nice being home with my husband and children. They needed me. But even more, I needed them. Also, I was afraid if I returned to the hospital, the doctors would find so many things wrong that they would keep me there.

I knew the Lord could remove that infection so we discussed it as a family. Each one of us said a prayer. Then the bishop came over and administered to me.

My temperature returned to normal, and my leg stopped oozing infection. The burning sensation around the pin stopped. The infection was gone. I did not have to return to the hospital.

The following April, almost seven months after the accident, I returned to the hospital for X-rays. It was determined that my leg had healed sufficiently for the pins to be removed so I could begin using crutches.

With the pins out, and the apparatus that held them rigid gone, I was able to roll onto my stomach for the first time in seven months. What a relief for my back, but I could only stay there a short time because it hurt so badly.

My hopes were high now that I was going to start using crutches. I could finally learn to walk, which meant I could begin taking care of my family again. My life would return to normal.

The physical therapist came to my hospital room to start working on my leg. Her objective was to get some kind of movement in the knee joint because it was as stiff as if there was no joint there. She was an extremely strong woman.

She pulled me into a sitting position and put my knees on the edge of the bed where she could have maximum leverage in forcing the stiff one to bend. With all her strength she would push, then relax, then push again. She continued this several times, again and again. Finally, I told her to stop that I couldn't take any more of the pain.

Instead of stopping, she gave one more hard push. Something cracked. We both heard it like a dry stick breaking. She said it was adhesion growths in my knee that had popped.

She pulled me off the bed into a standing position. I almost fainted right there, the pain was so intense. Later X-rays showed that she had shattered my thigh bone, and by making me stand had pushed the shattered point of the lower bone up into the marrow of the larger bone above.

I didn't know the physical body could stand so much pain. No amount of medication was strong enough to relieve those terrible spasms of pain. For two days I could not use the bed pan, and for five days I could not eat. The following Monday, they put my leg in traction, finally relieving the spasms. On Tuesday they rolled me into surgery and put the pins back in my leg, in different places, drilling new holes.

My world crashed around me. I was starting all over again. I didn't know if I could bear another seven months on my back waiting for my leg to heal a second time. I was devastated.

I reached out for anything that might give me comfort. I couldn't stand it any more. I prayed again and again. I needed comfort. I needed strength. I felt so lost, and forgotten.

I picked up the *Doctrine and Covenants,* praying the book would open to a place that would help me. The book opened to section 58, where I read the following:

> 2 For verily I say unto you, blessed is he
> that keepeth my commandments,
> whether in life or in death; and he that is
> faithful in tribulation, the reward of the
> same is greater in the kingdom of heaven.
> 3 Ye cannot behold with your natural
> eyes, for the present time, the design of
> your God concerning those things which
> shall come hereafter, and the glory which
> shall follow after much tribulation.
> 4 For after much tribulation come the
> blessings. Wherefore the day cometh that
> ye shall be crowned with much glory; the
> hour is not yet, but is nigh at hand.

It seemed these words came straight from heaven to me. The words and the feeling that came with them was the comfort I needed. These verses somehow filled that empty cavity in my heart. I read them over and over again.

The doctors told me that because of the second break, it was necessary to overlap the bone ends for strength. When it healed the broken leg would be much shorter than the other, and I would never have any bend in the knee. I would not have any more therapy treatments, and I would not be able to walk.

I have often worried about that therapist and how she might have felt. I have also worried about what she might think I was feeling toward her. Even with all the pain that I felt I could not hold any feelings against her. I forgave her completely in my heart and wanted her to know, but she never came back into my room.

Slowly, my leg healed a second time. While recovering I was overjoyed with each step of progress. I was thankful for each new thing I learned to do. I remember the first batch of dishes I washed while sitting in the wheelchair. I pulled up along the side of the sink and sat there crying with thankfulness.

The promise I was given at the time of the accident was kept. Not only did I live to raise my children, but I gave birth to three more. I regained use of my knee, and eventually learned to walk again.

For many, many years I did not share my out of body experience with anyone except my husband. As my children grew older, they learned of it. With the recent publication of many of these kinds of stories, I have felt strength and have desired to help others by sharing my experience as they have helped me by sharing theirs.

These many years have not dimmed this experience. It is very vivid. I recall the incidents and I recall the feelings. I would never like to endure again the terrible pain I went through, but I'm very thankful for that total experience. I thank my Heavenly Father for it. For some reason I needed the lessons of physical pain.

Especially now with the recent passing of my husband, I look so forward to the marvelous day when I die again, this time for good. I know that death is a beautiful, wondrous and glorious experience. It is nothing to fear.